Rise Luminosity

"Your eyes should meet Nature's eyes"

Anil Annaiah

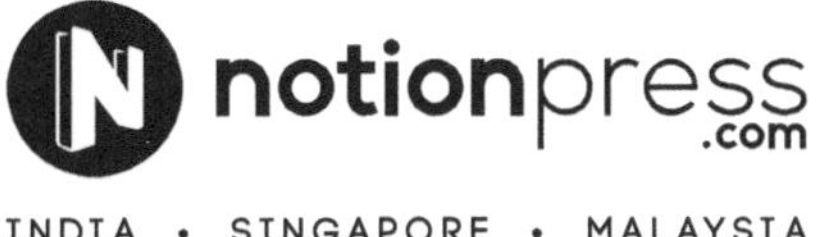

INDIA • SINGAPORE • MALAYSIA

ISBN 979-8-89724-507-9

This book has been published with all efforts taken to make the material error-free after the consent of the author. However, the author and the publisher do not assume and hereby disclaim any liability to any party for any loss, damage, or disruption caused by errors or omissions, whether such errors or omissions result from negligence, accident, or any other cause.

While every effort has been made to avoid any mistake or omission, this publication is being sold on the condition and understanding that neither the author nor the publishers or printers would be liable in any manner to any person by reason of any mistake or omission in this publication or for any action taken or omitted to be taken or advice rendered or accepted on the basis of this work. For any defect in printing or binding the publishers will be liable only to replace the defective copy by another copy of this work then available.

Find Images and Words inside which can open the Mind.

Twisting Words... True Meanings

From the Author of Nobody Speaks To Me, Simple Perceptions, My Mirror, New Clouds, Open Windows, Our Horizons, Tiny Pathways, Wide Canvas & The Starburst.

To My Son

Arav

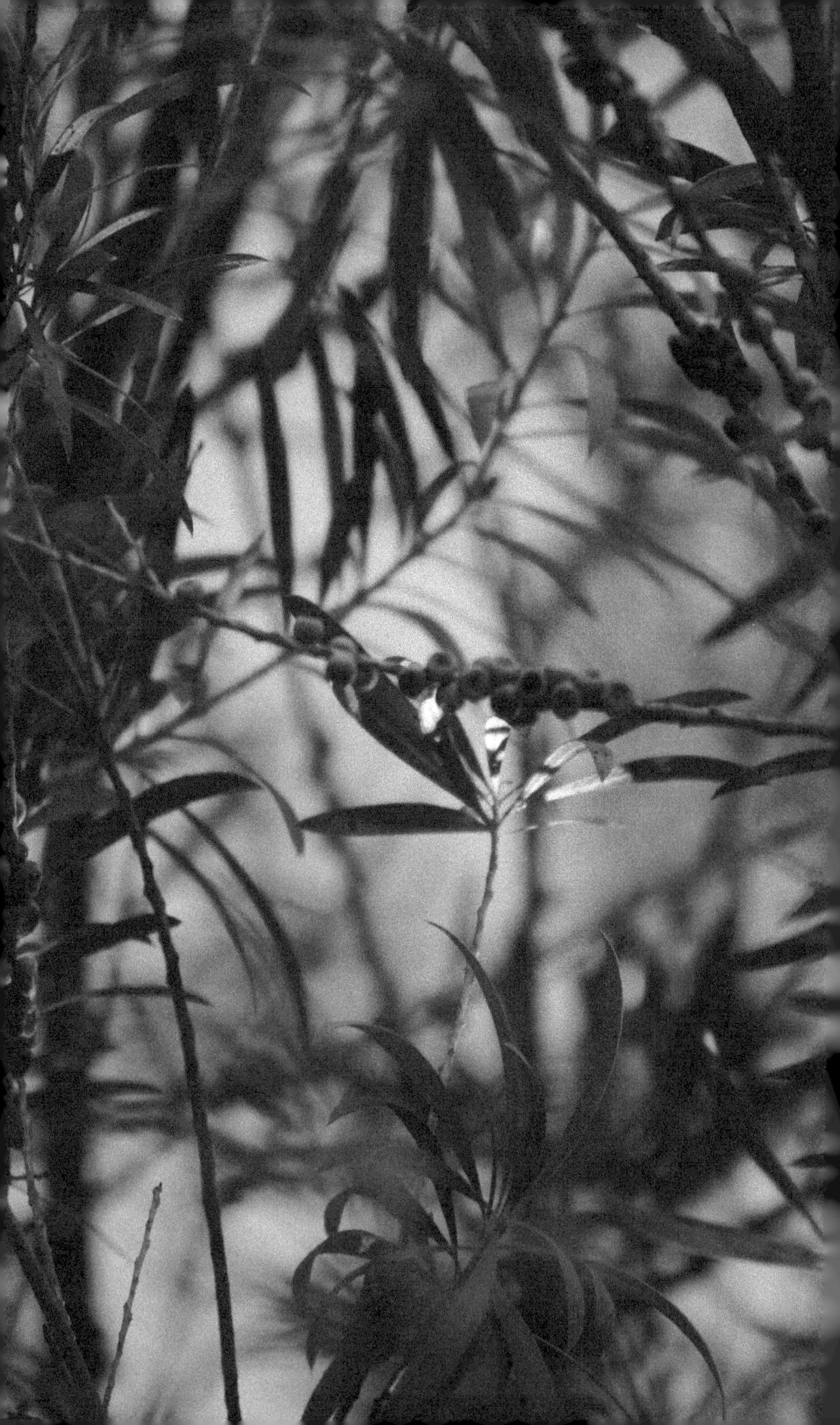

Preface

I present my Tenth book "Rise Luminosity" with more thoughts for you to ponder upon.

This comes after my Nine books with thoughts presented as "Nobody Speaks To Me", "Simple Perceptions", "My Mirror", "New Clouds", "Open Windows", "Our Horizons", "Tiny Pathways", "Wide Canvas" & "The Starburst".

In the book "Rise Luminosity" the words are about elevating your mind to resonate with the deepest desires of the universe. The book presents thoughts that can assist you to align yourself better in your quest to find happiness.

Writing these new set of thoughts over time, has been a process of revelation and an adventure with words as always. These strings of words emerge from the observation of humanity.

The images in this book add another dimension for you to explore. The images remain close to the words and offer a sense of conceptualism.

I believe in words, they have a force and power, strong enough to change destinies.

My faith in words keeps me delving towards writing more.

Anil Annaiah

Words can give us courage to
overcome... the gusty winds.

Words can give us the strength to
swim... the rising tides.

Words can help us celebrate... the
power of human kindness.

Words... can help us fulfil our
dream... for a better world.

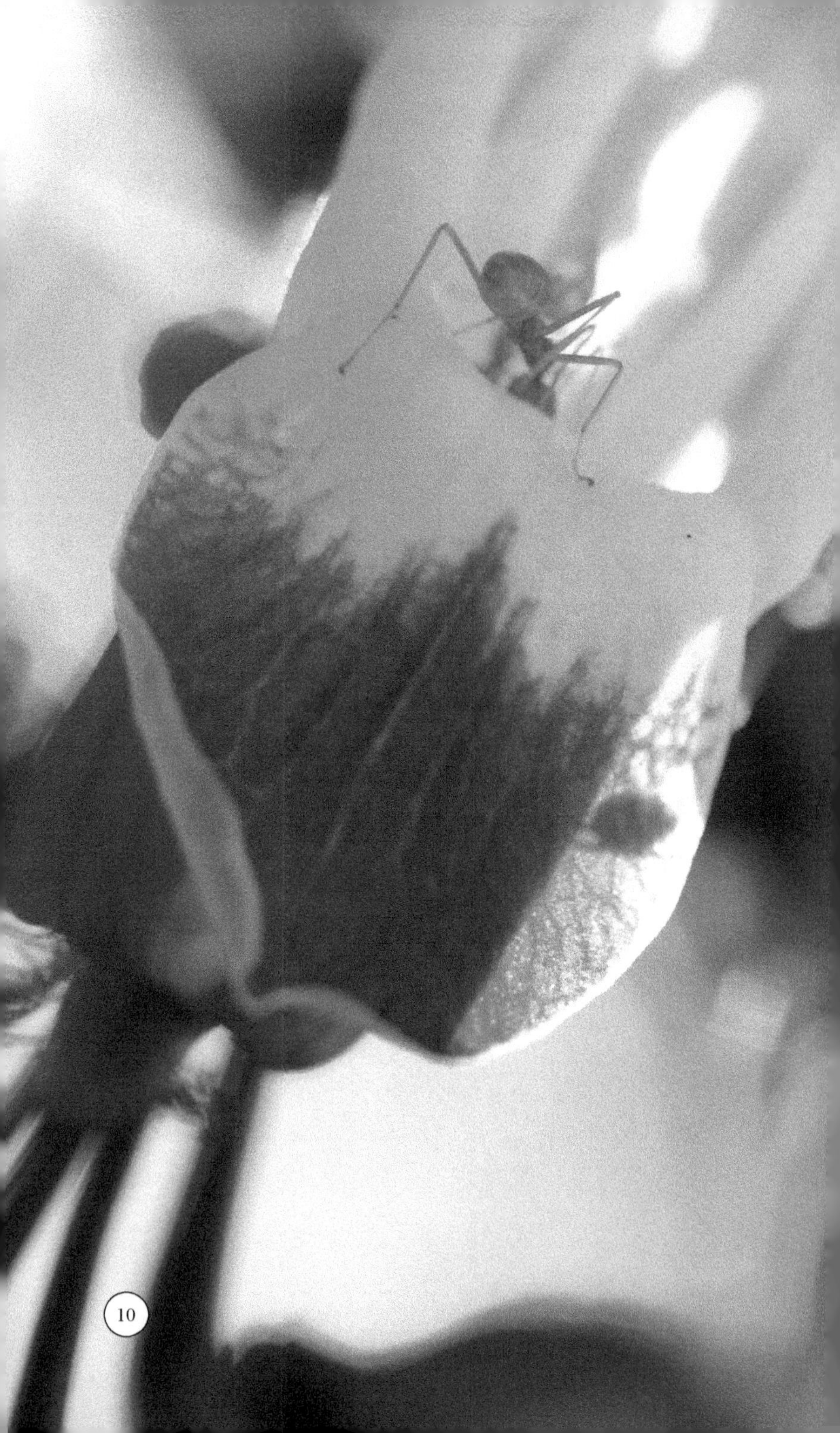

**Reaffirmations...
and irrelevance
meet often.**

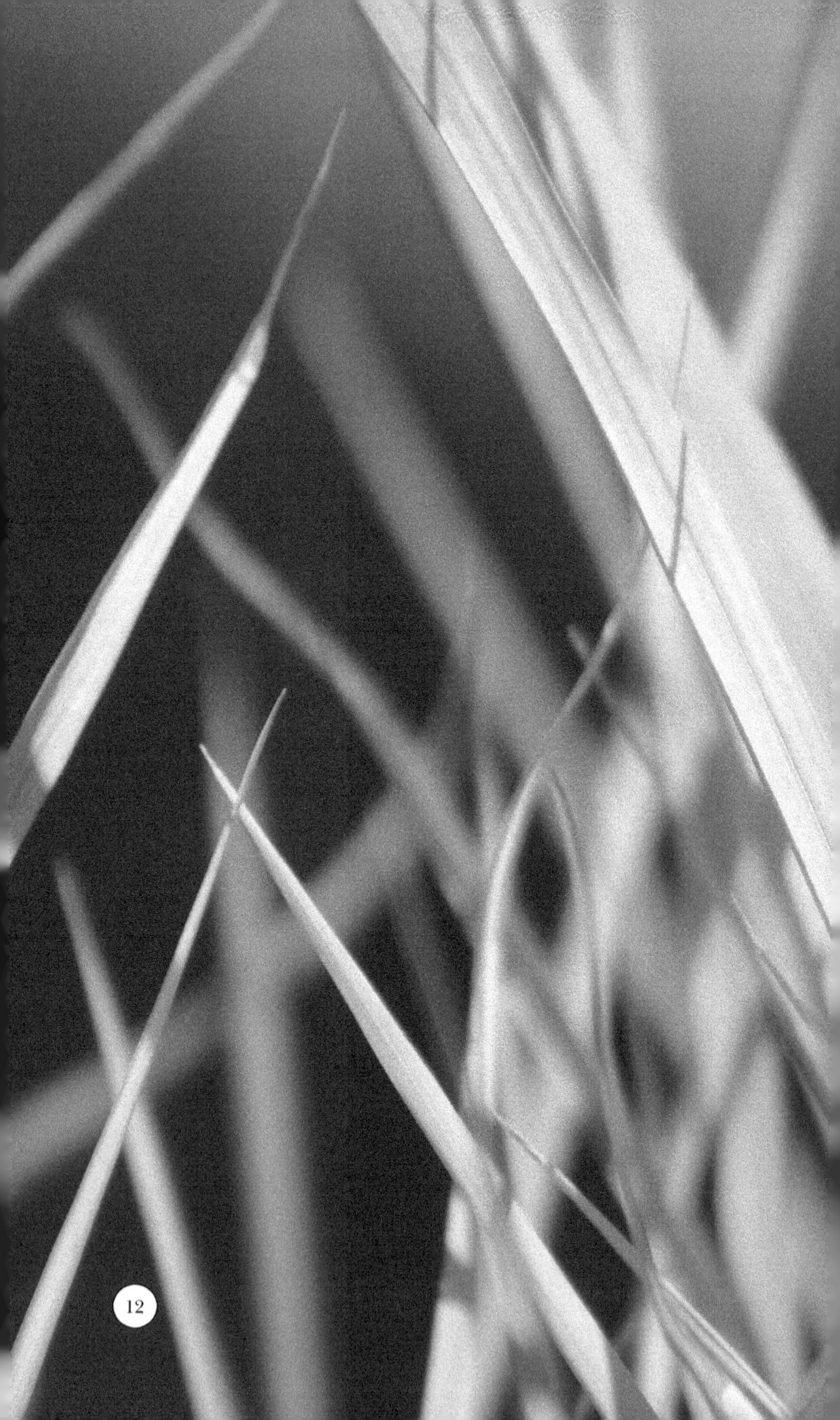

If only you could... sail through the veils... of distractions.

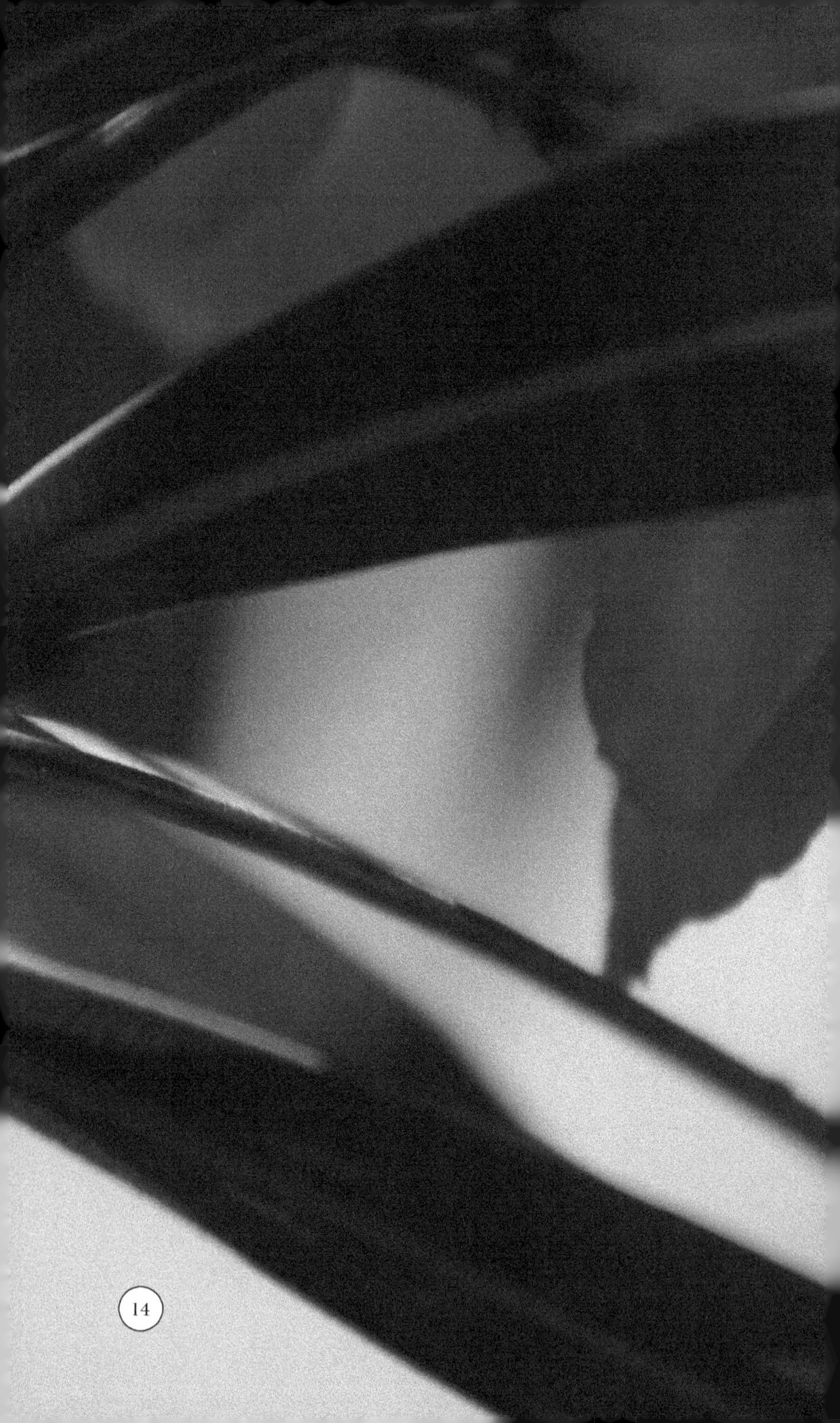

We are all here to falter... unless we hold on to strong reins.

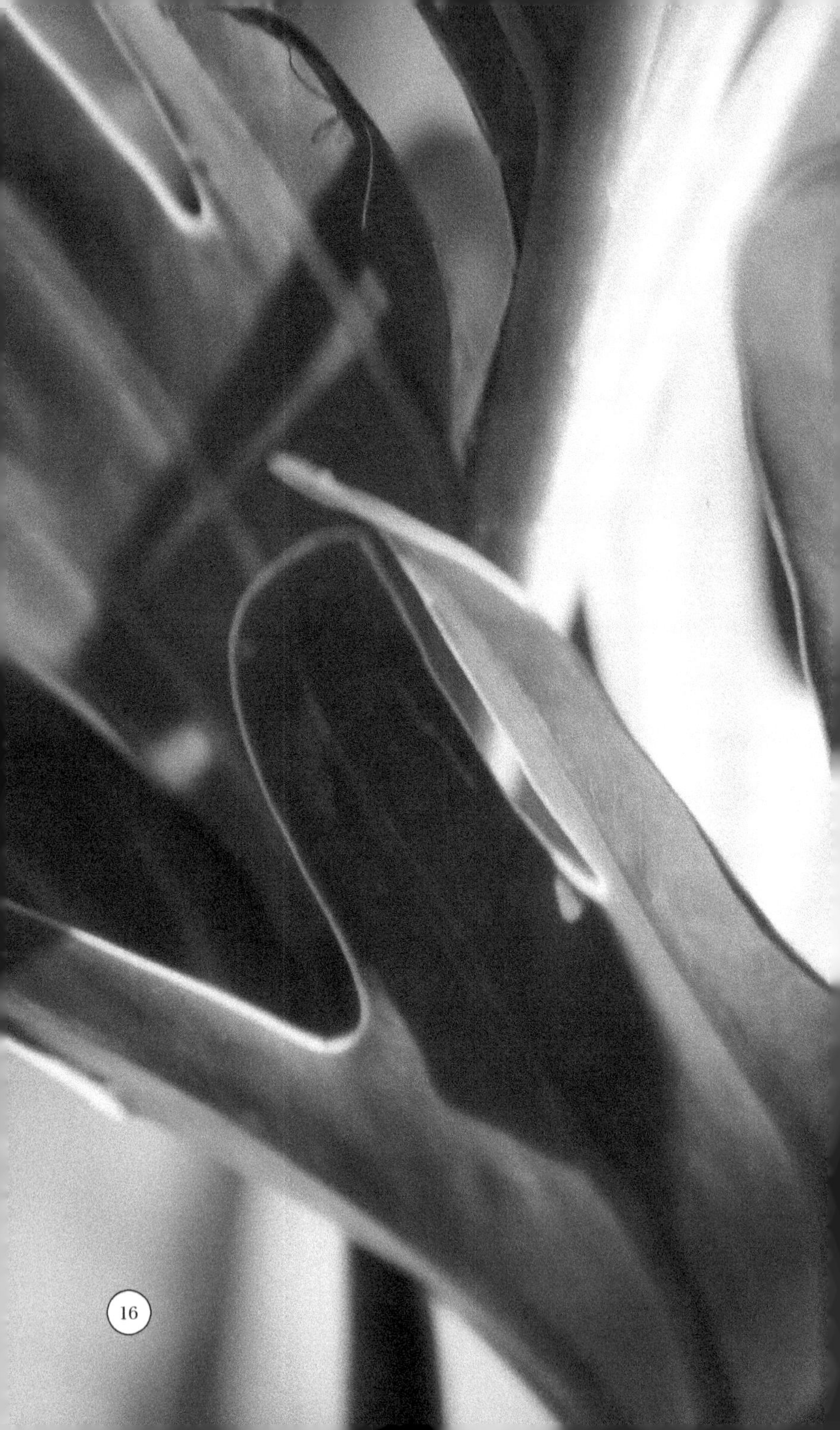

Invite forgiveness...
into your fold.

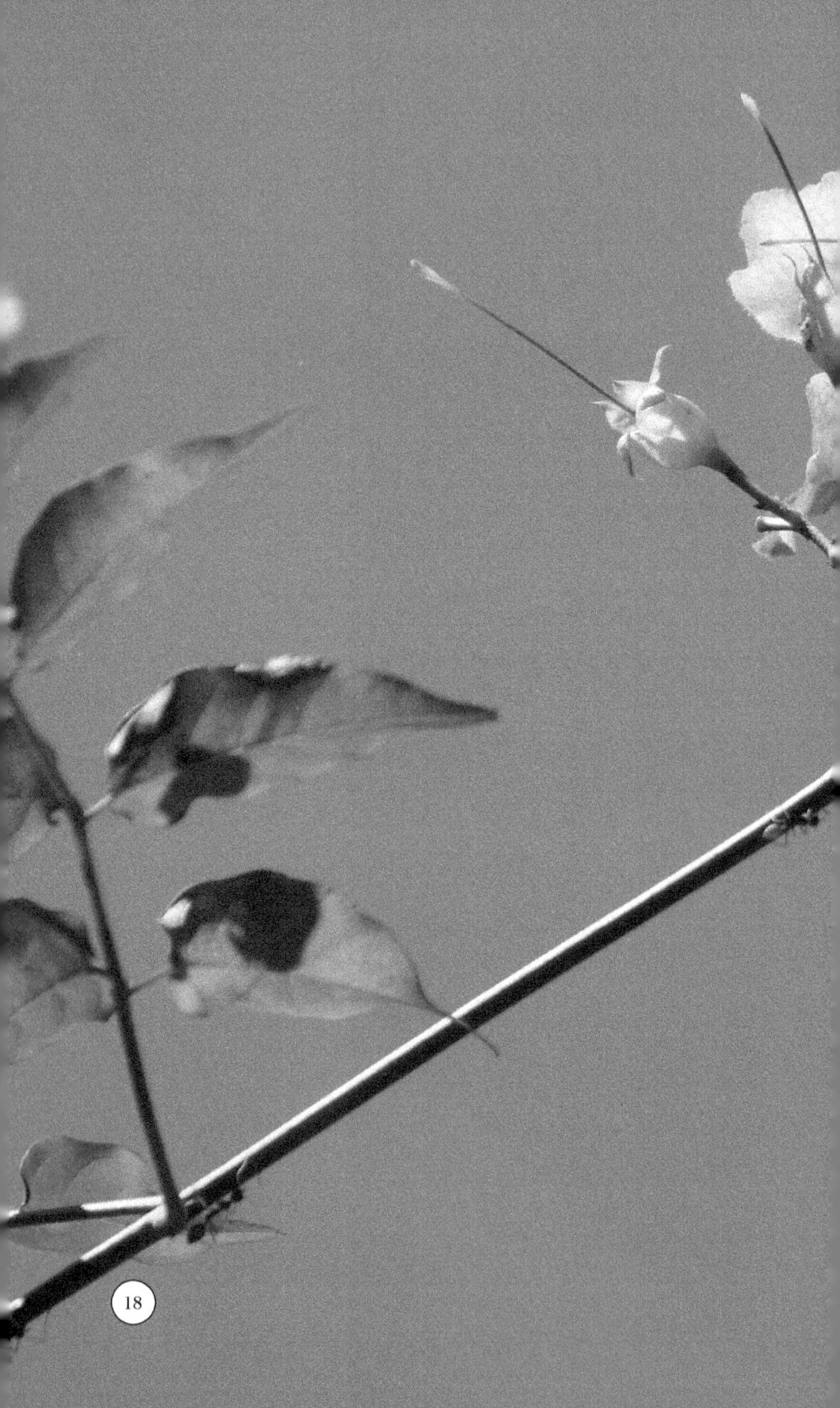

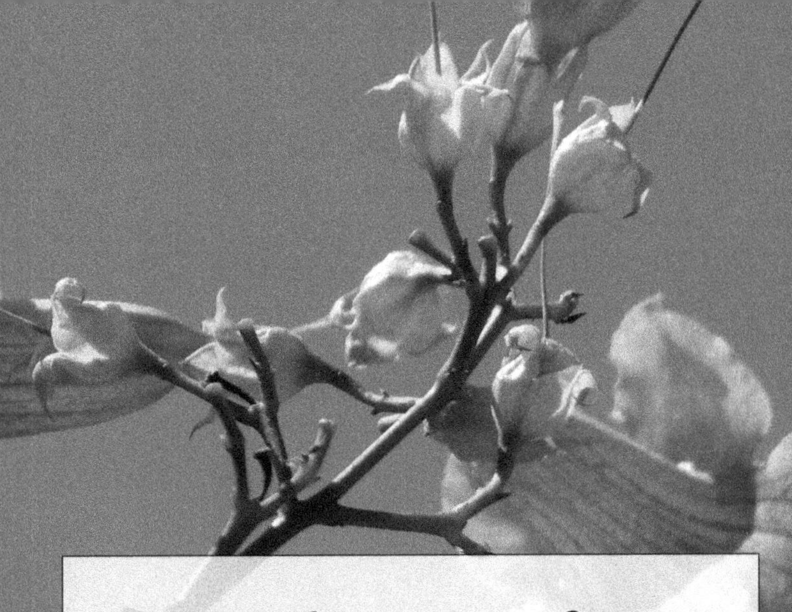

Do not let go... of your pristine resolve... when your body needs it the most.

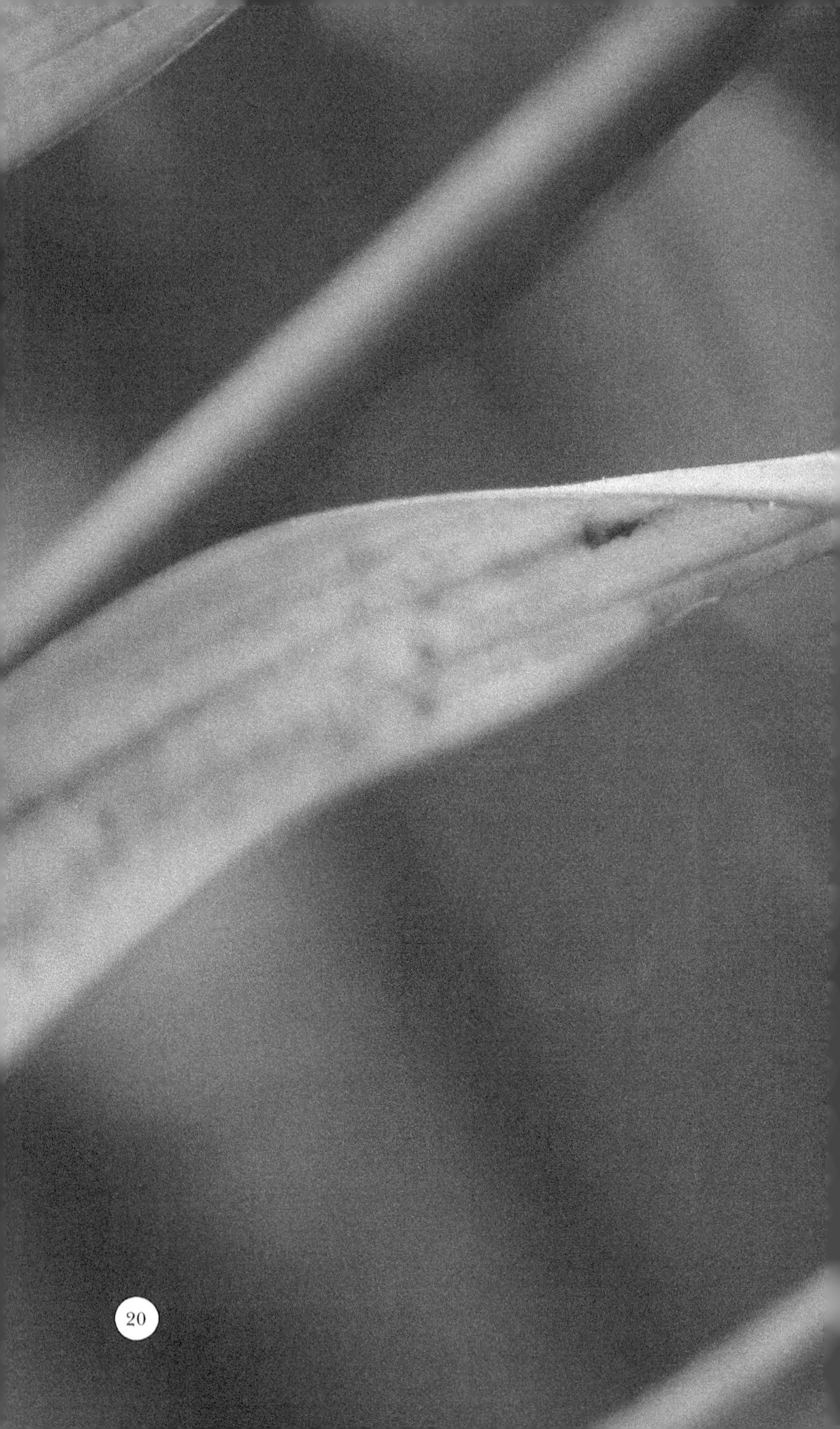

Ask yourself... most of the questions... and less of others.

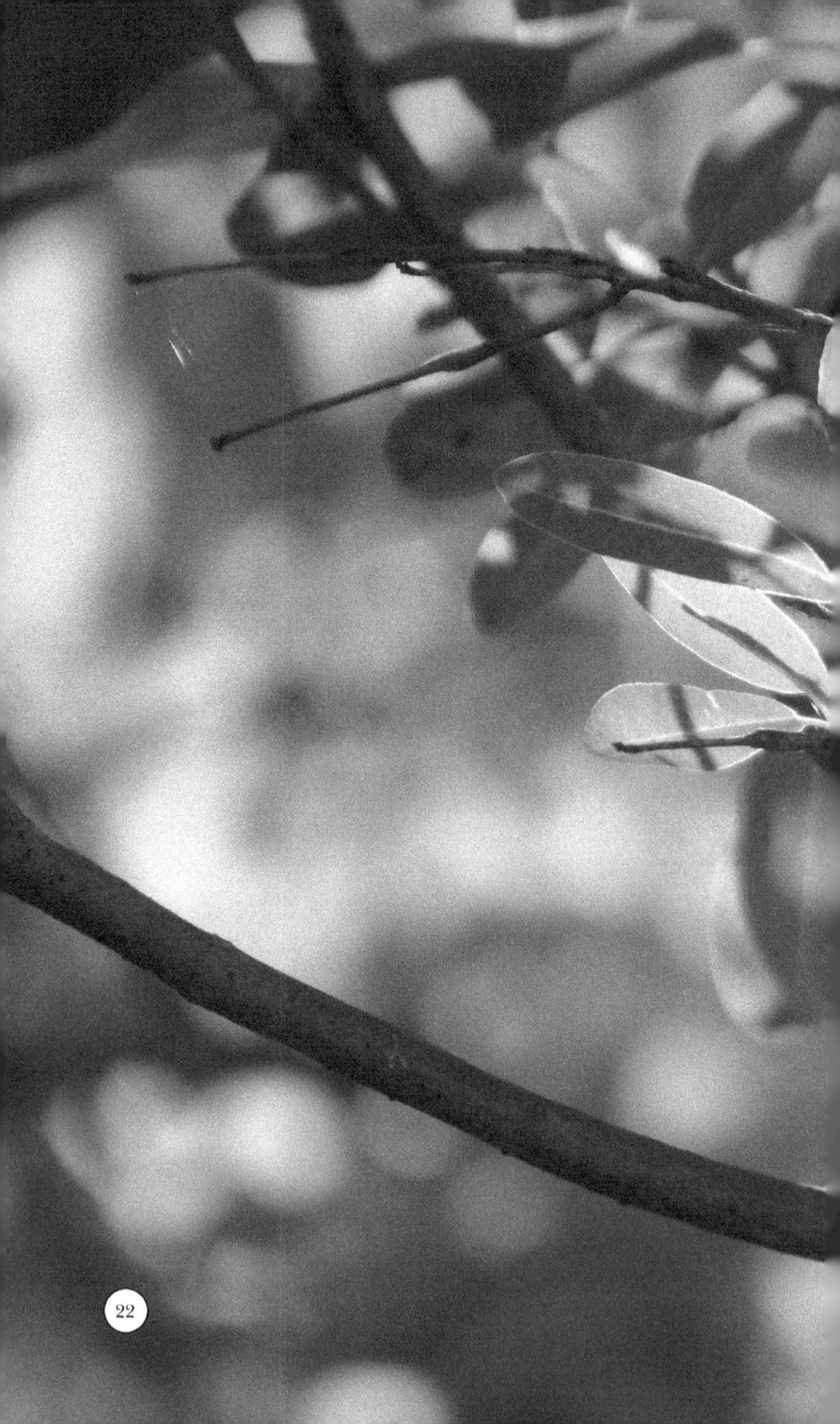

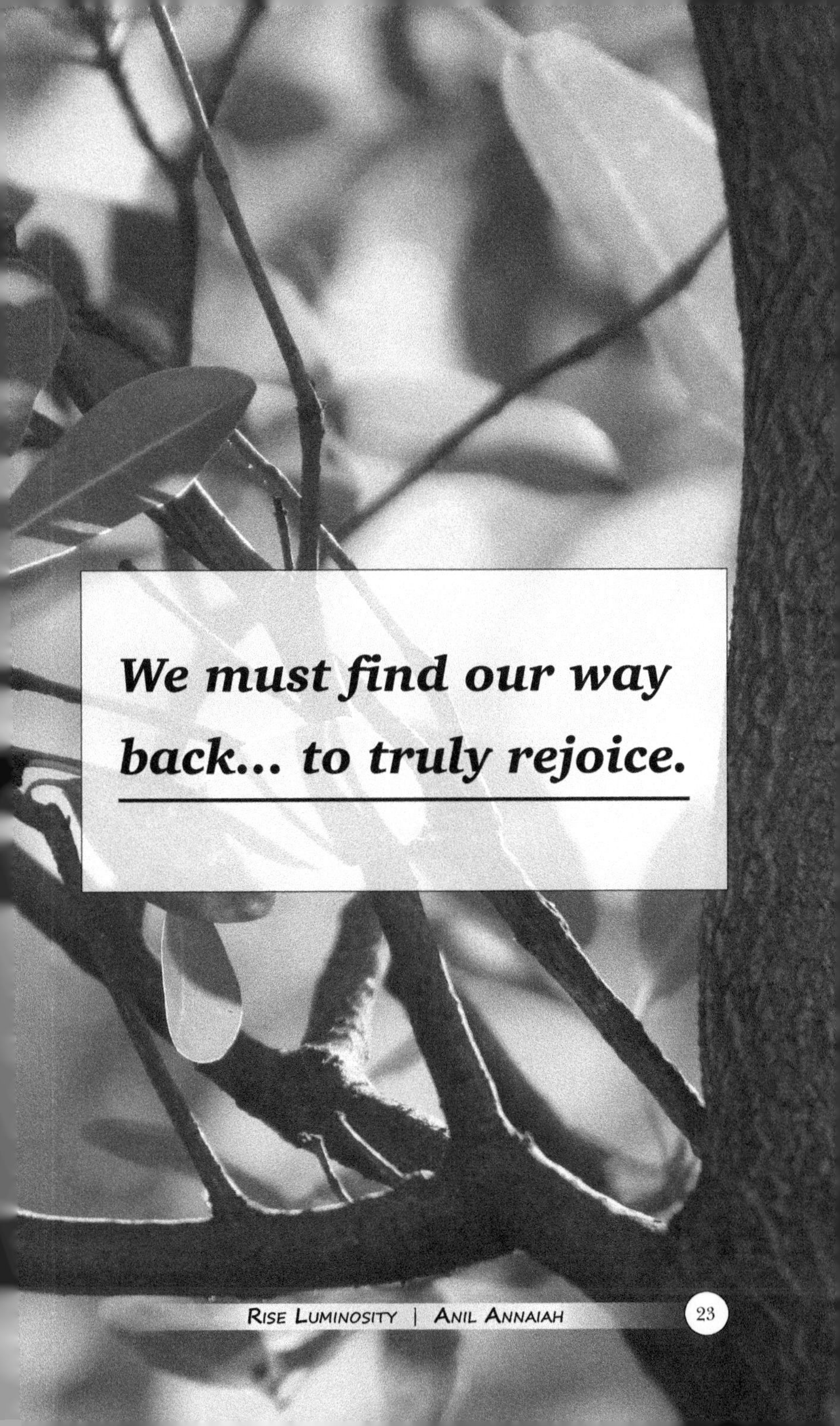

We must find our way back... to truly rejoice.

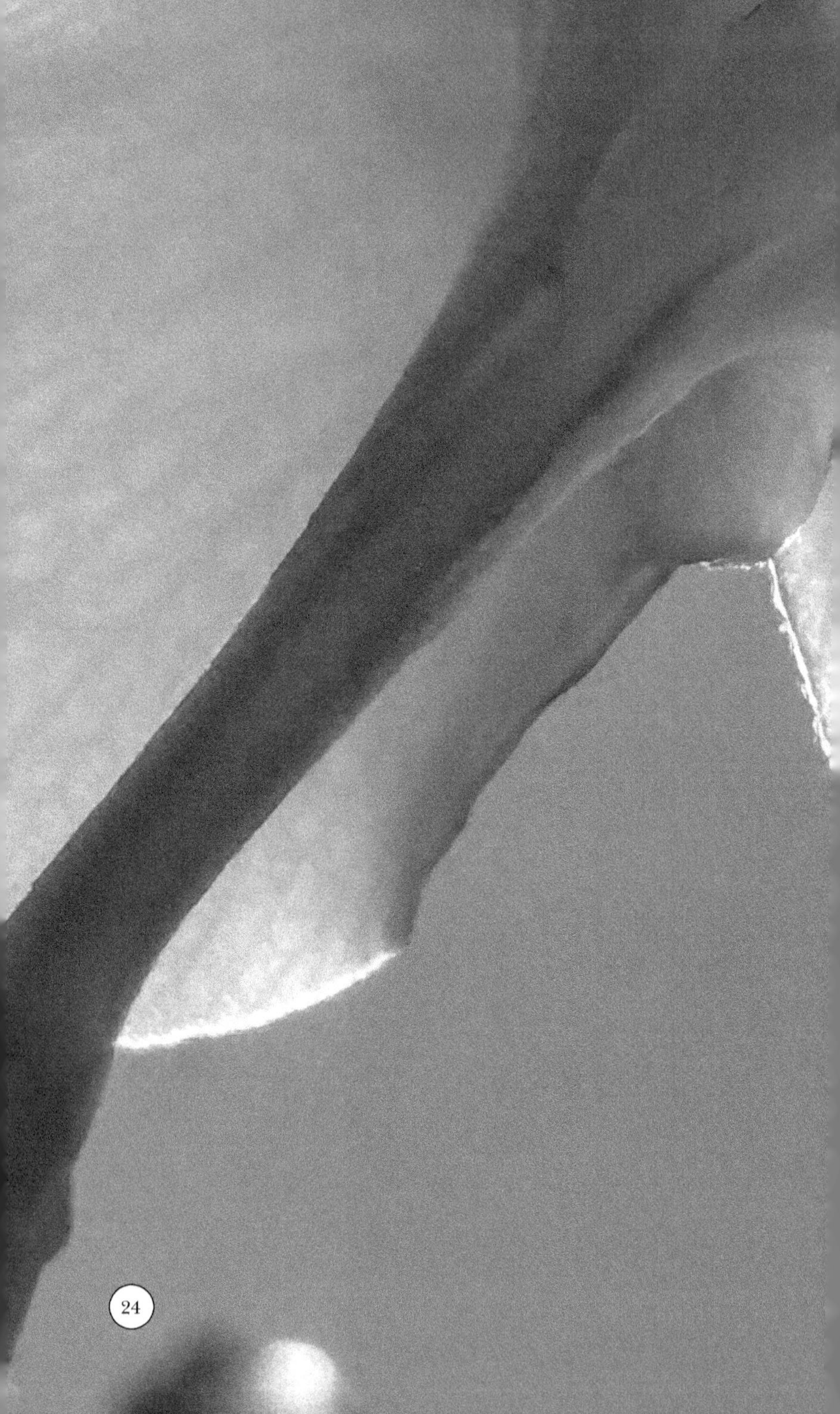
24

We periodically...
get pinned down by
blindness.

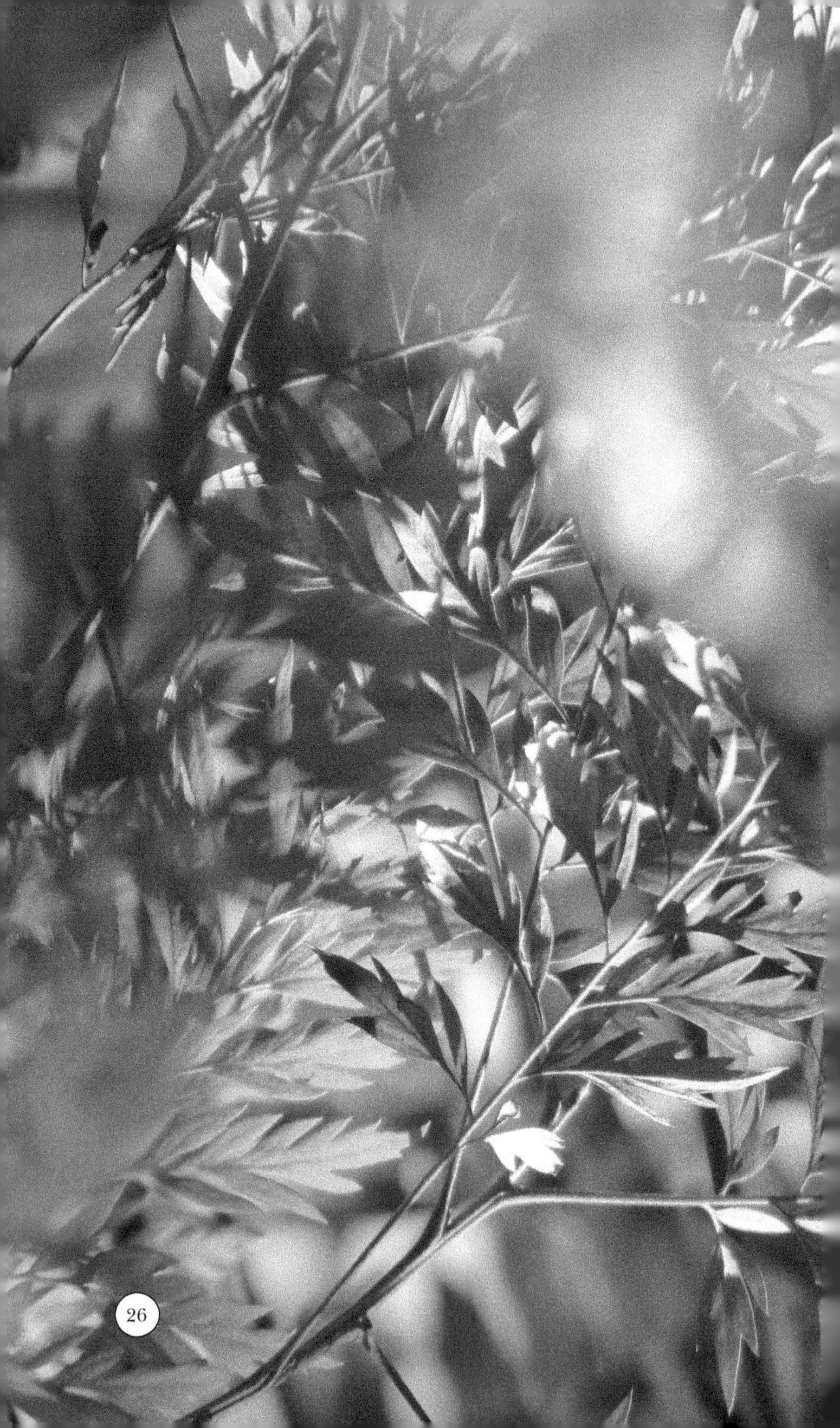

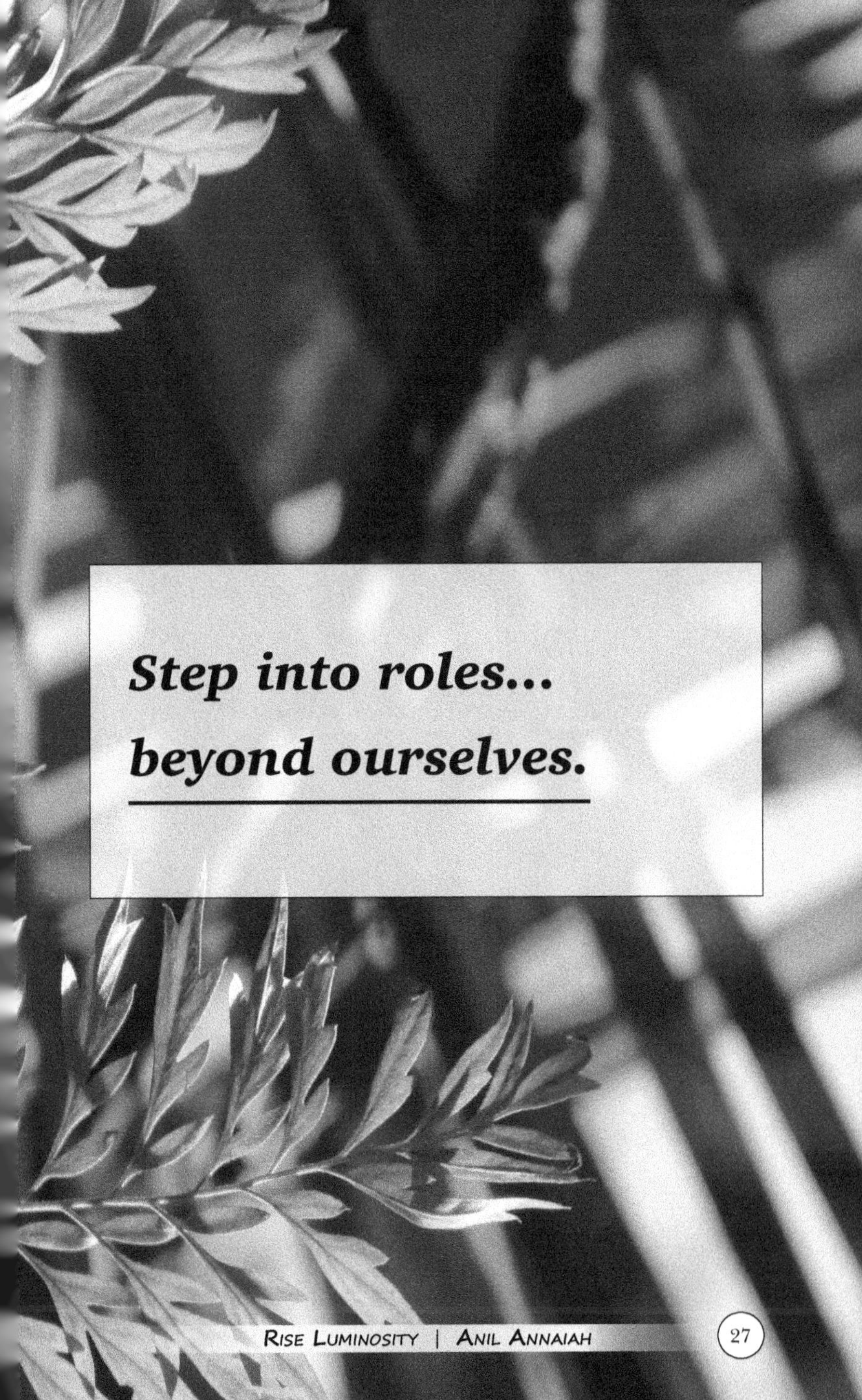

Step into roles...
beyond ourselves.

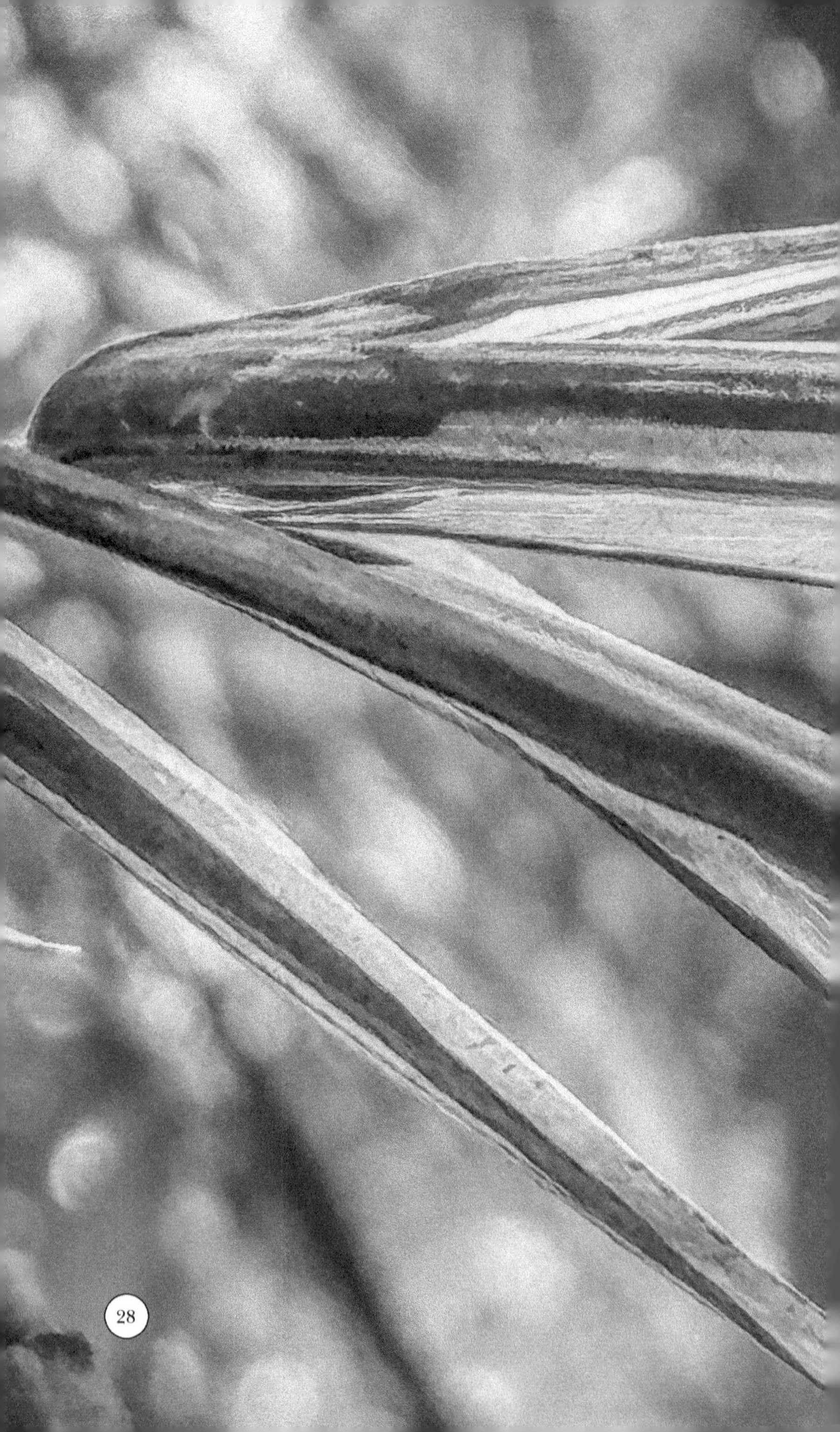

We have to follow silence... but not with timidity.

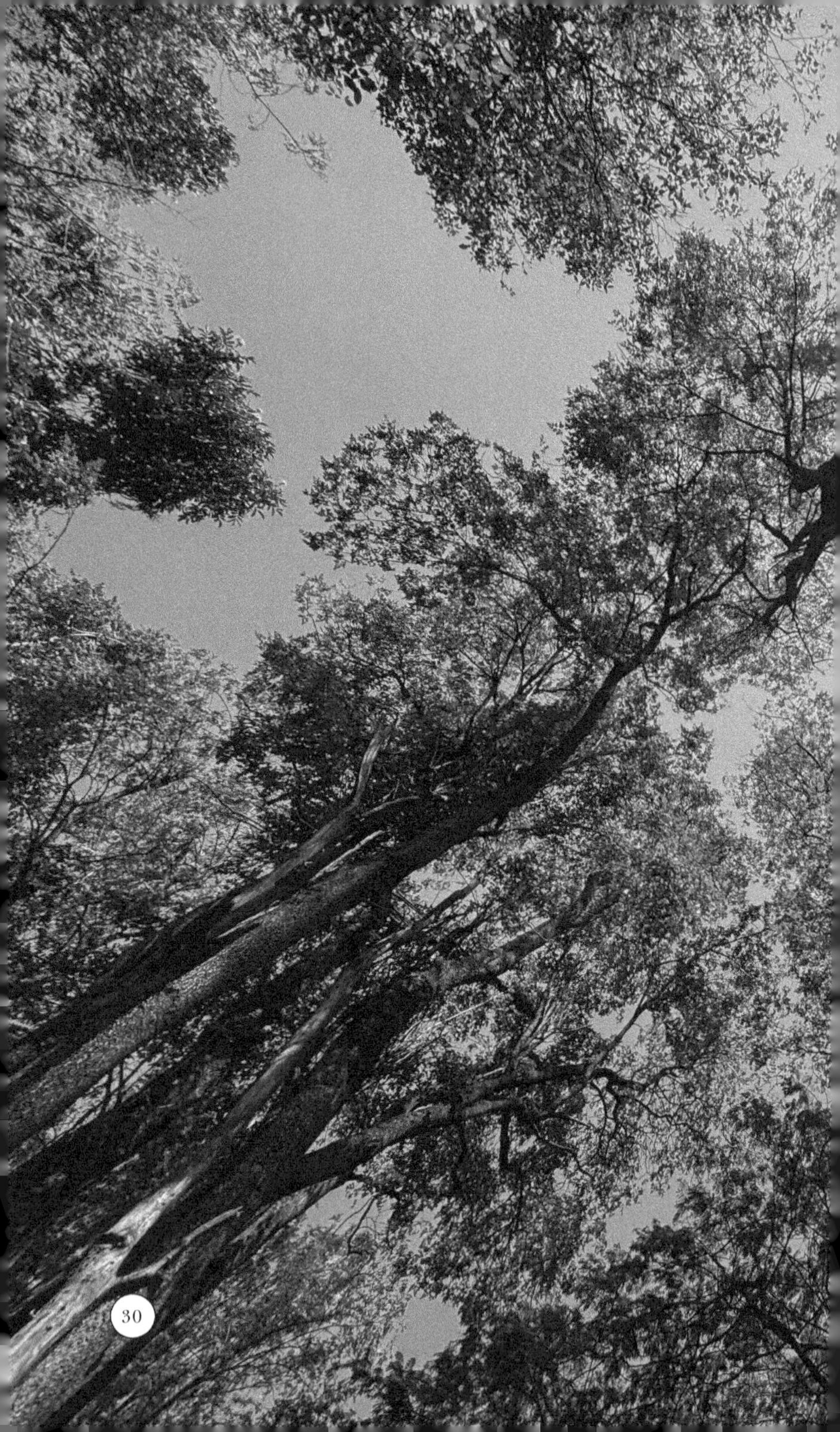

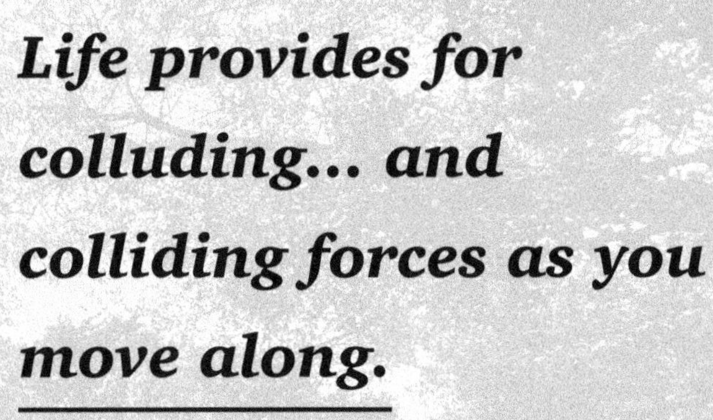

Life provides for colluding... and colliding forces as you move along.

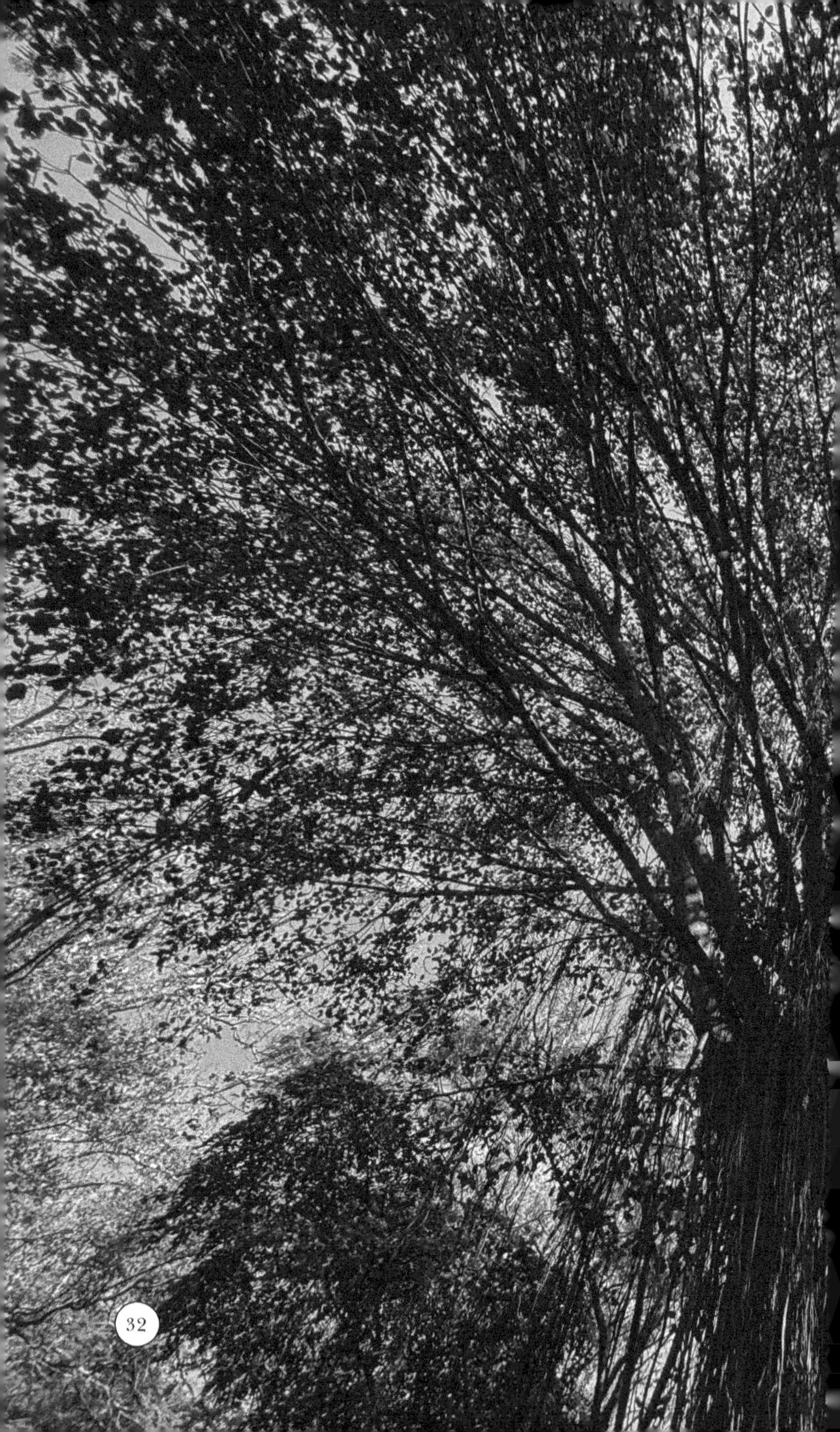

Silently your anxieties... will find ways to guide you.

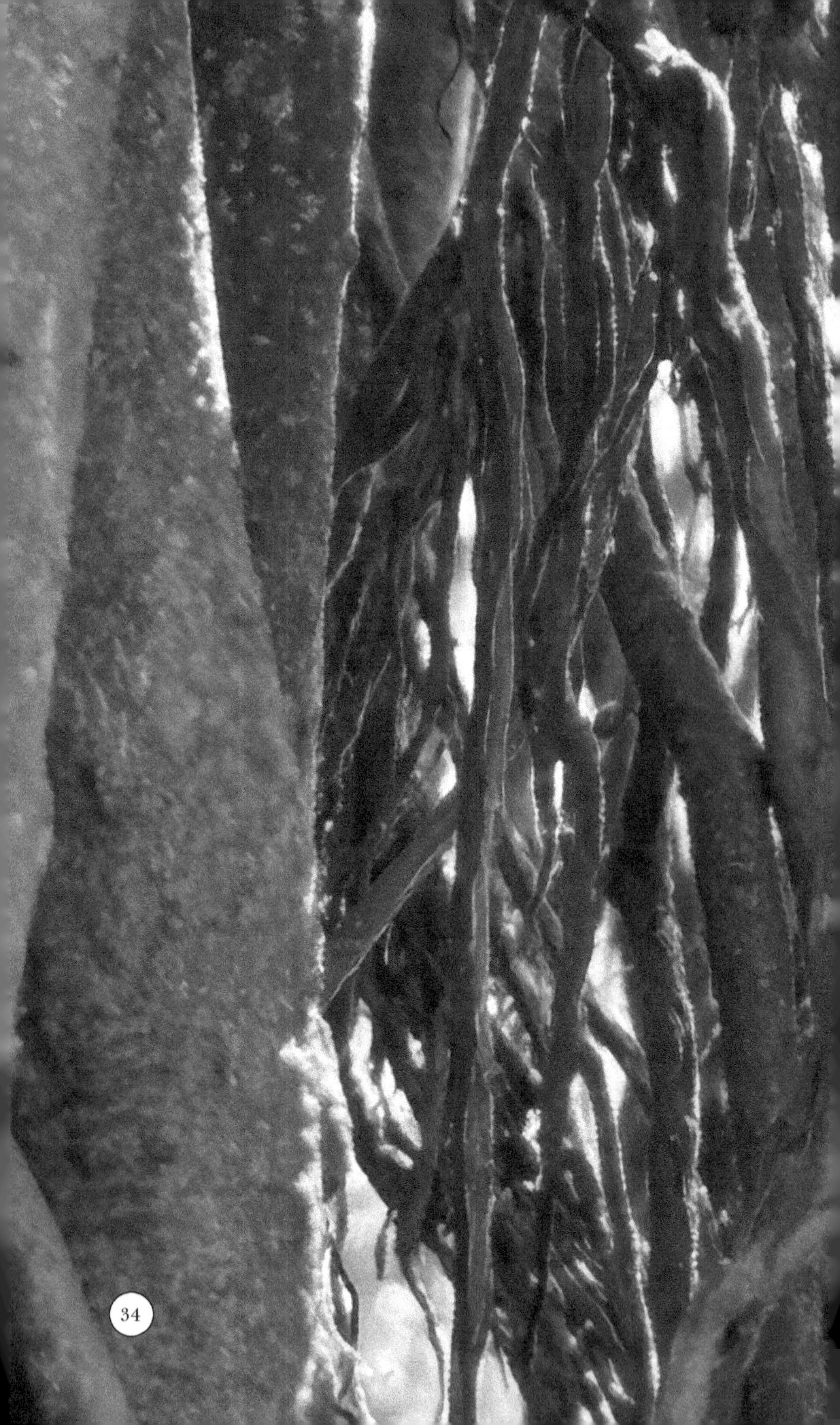

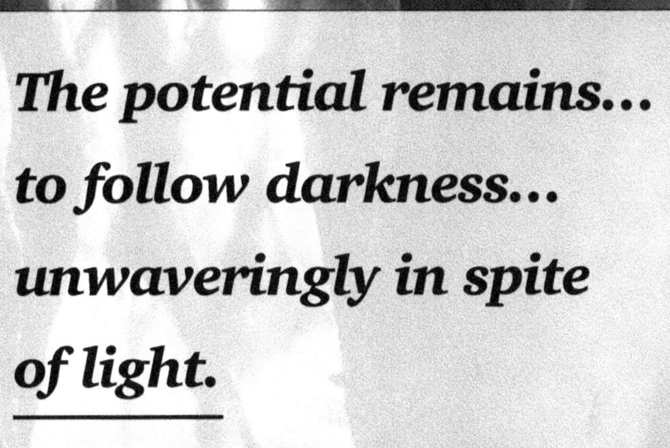

The potential remains...
to follow darkness...
unwaveringly in spite
of light.

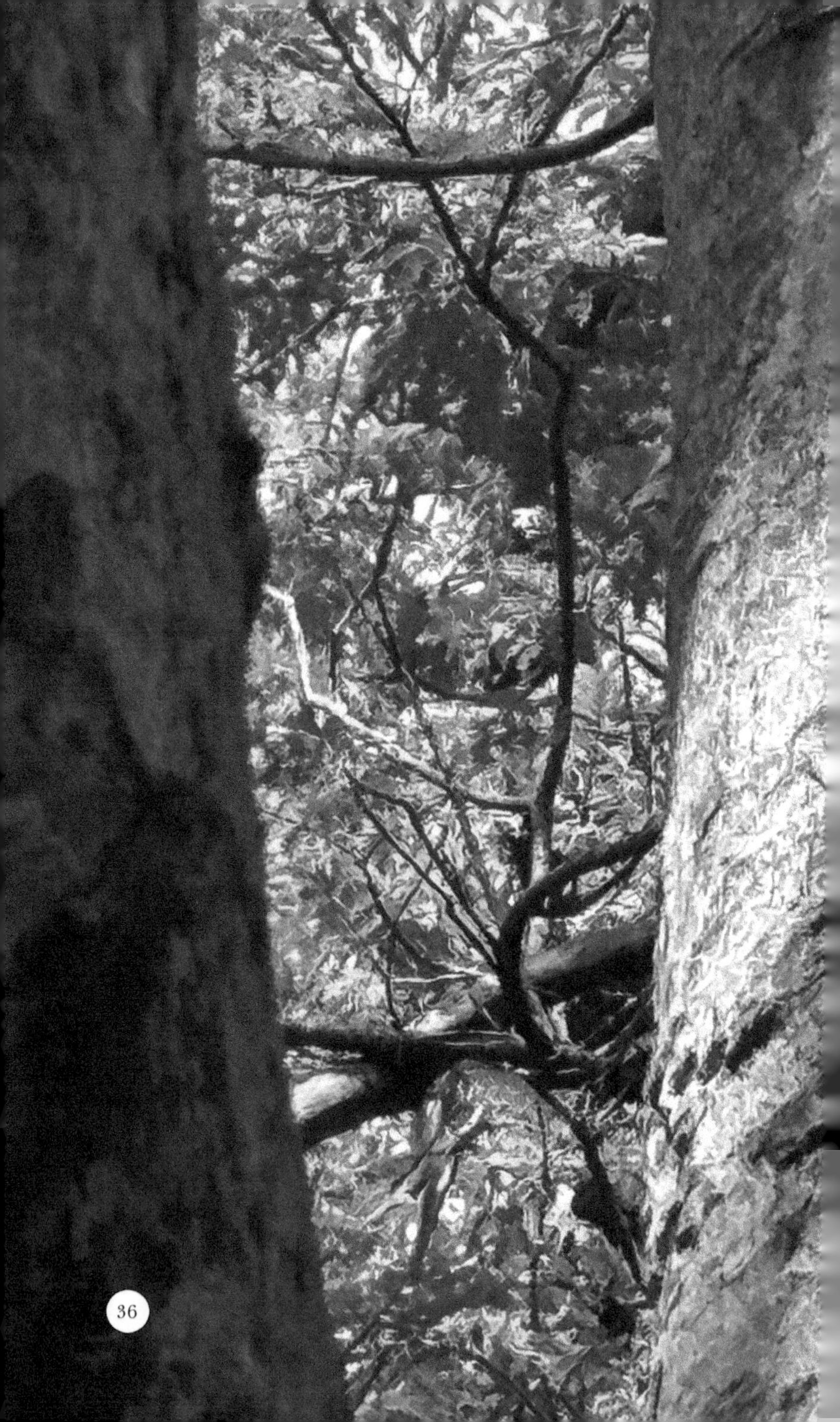

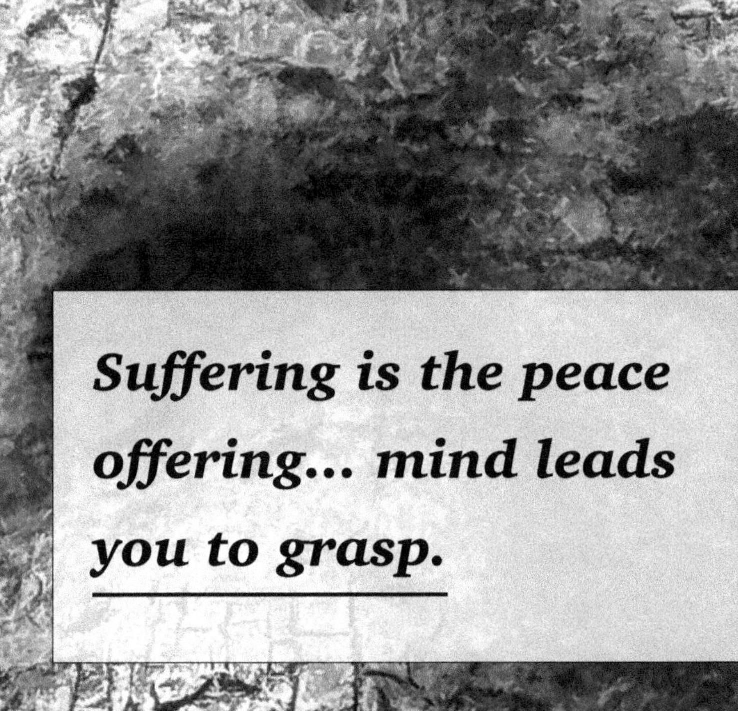

Suffering is the peace offering... mind leads you to grasp.

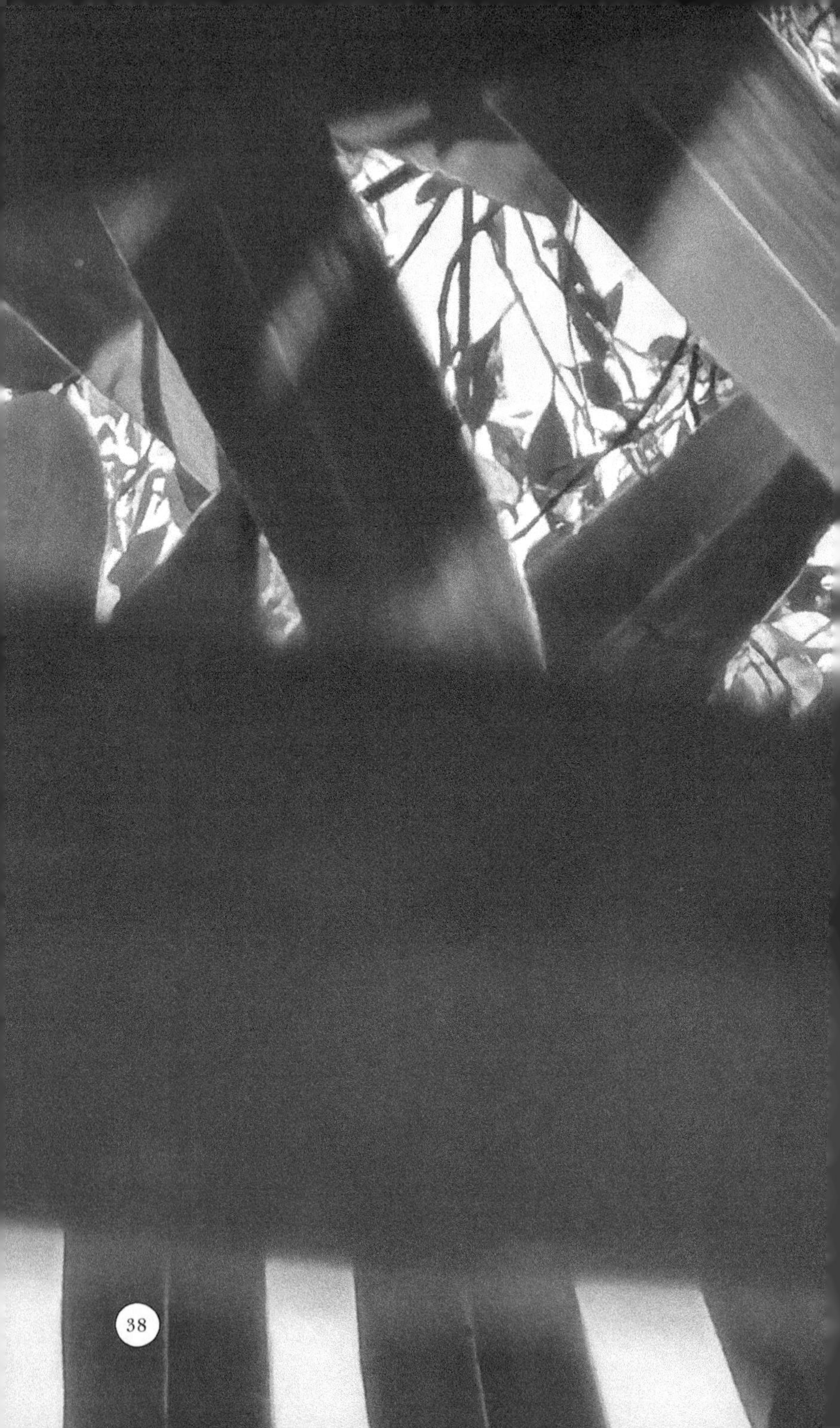

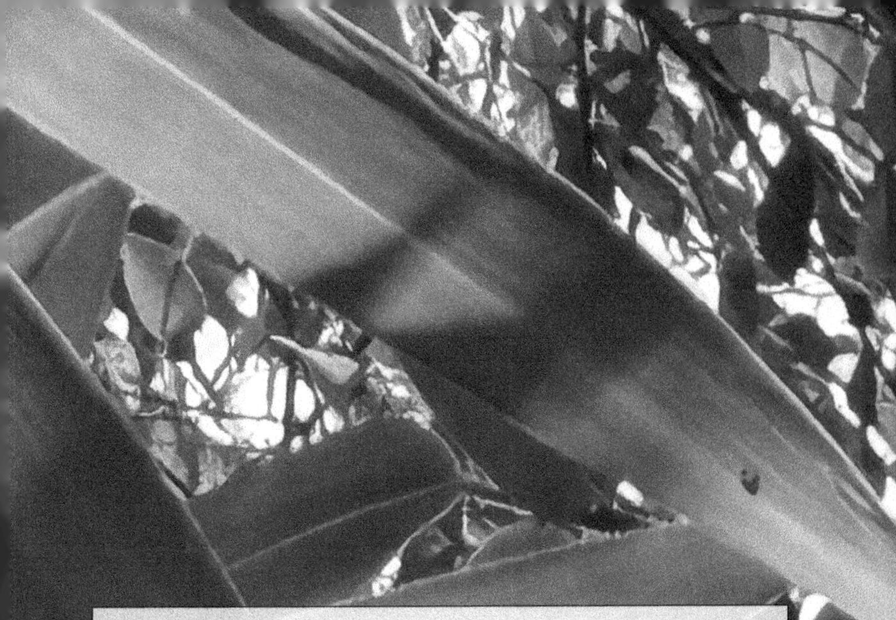

Assurances... or reassurances are none... in your life path.

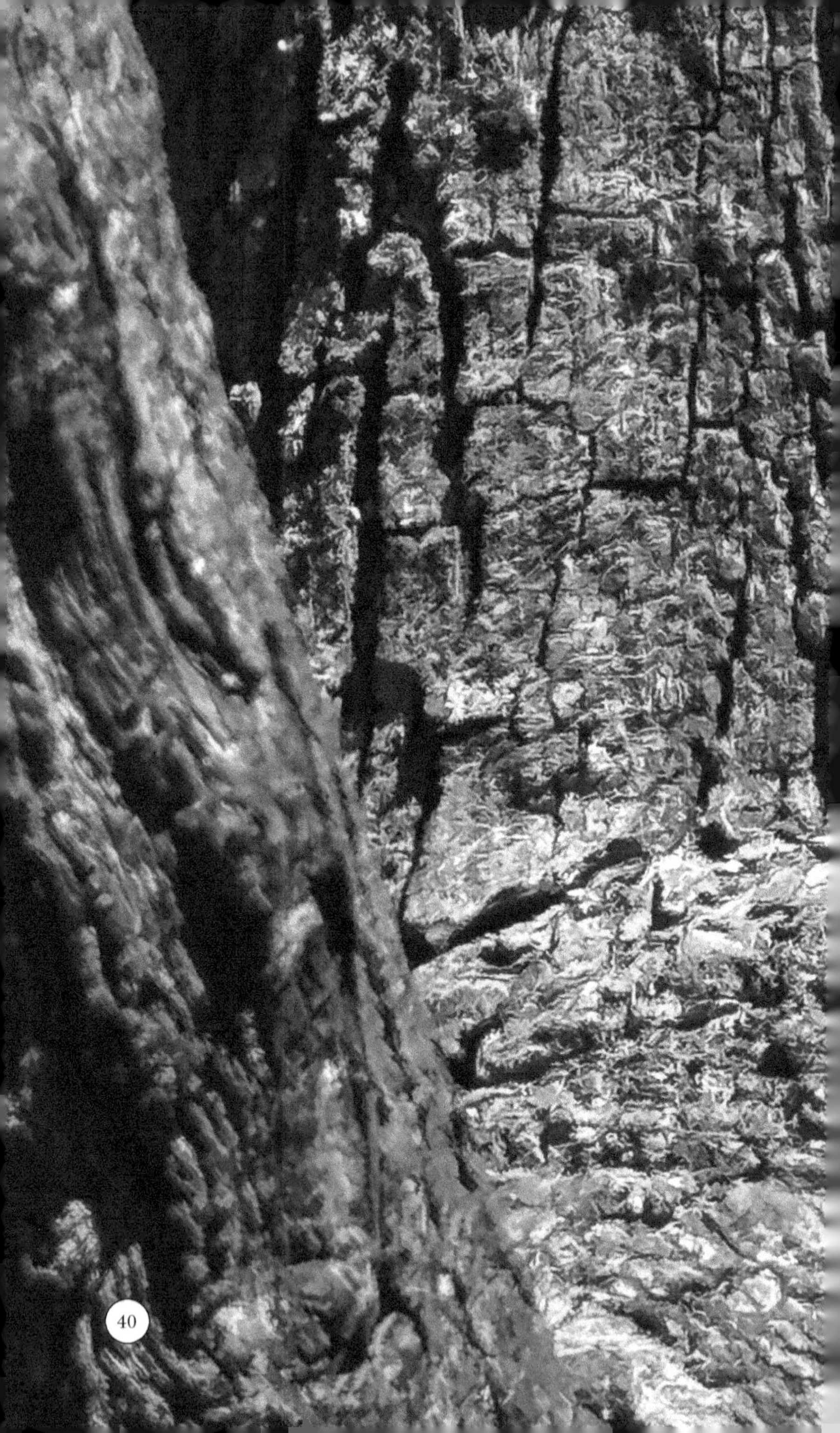

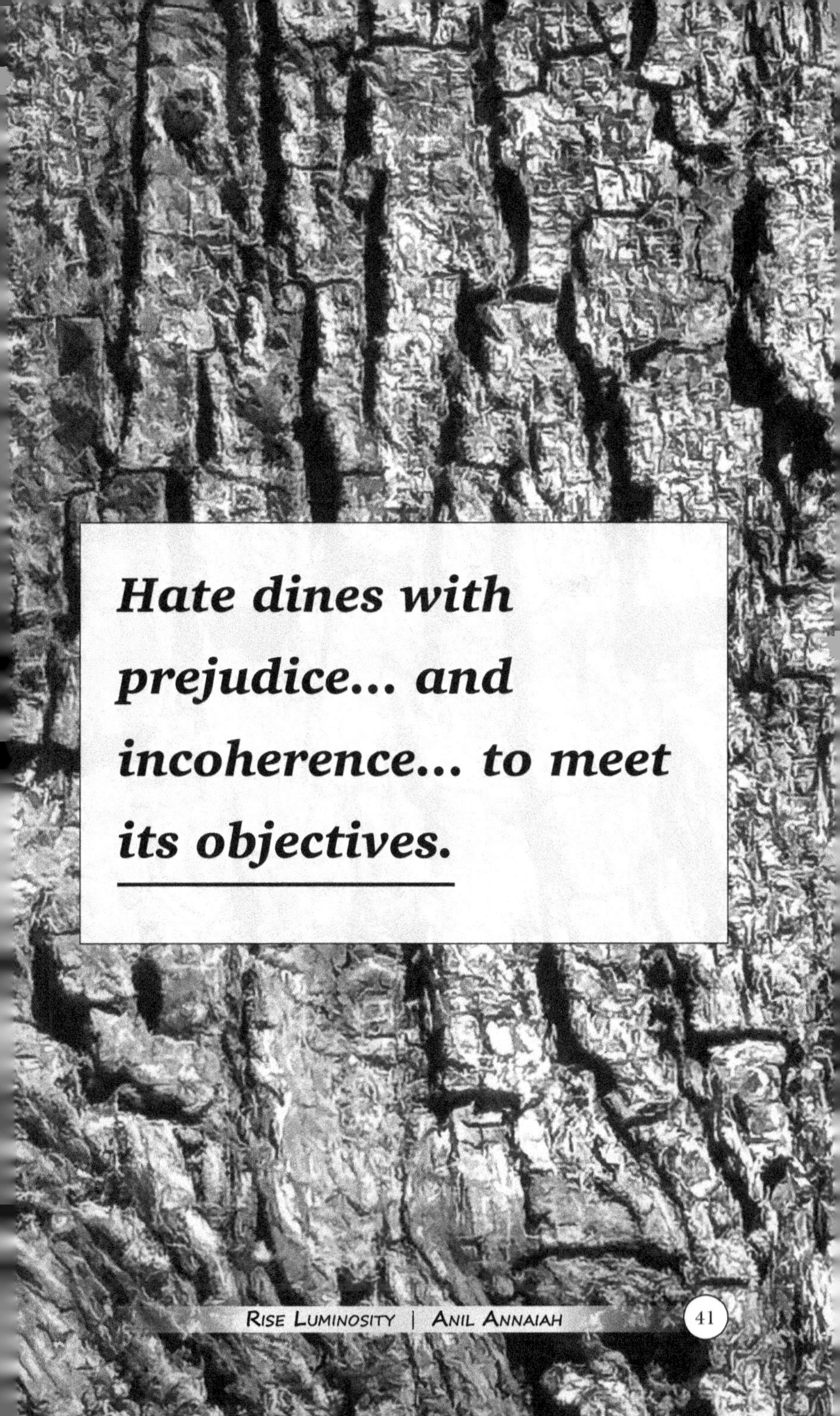

Hate dines with prejudice... and incoherence... to meet its objectives.

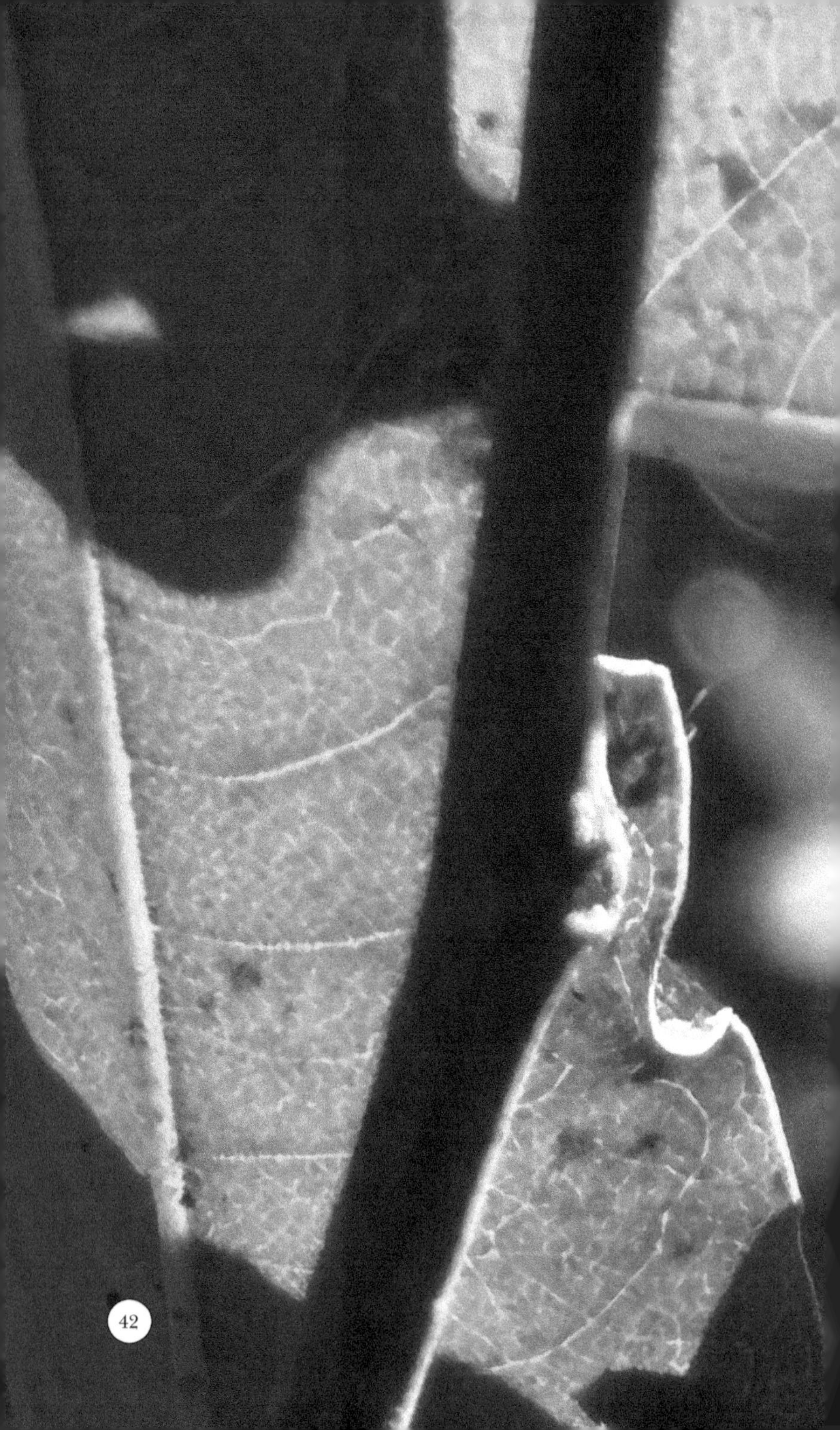

Can you be fair to all... and unfair to none.

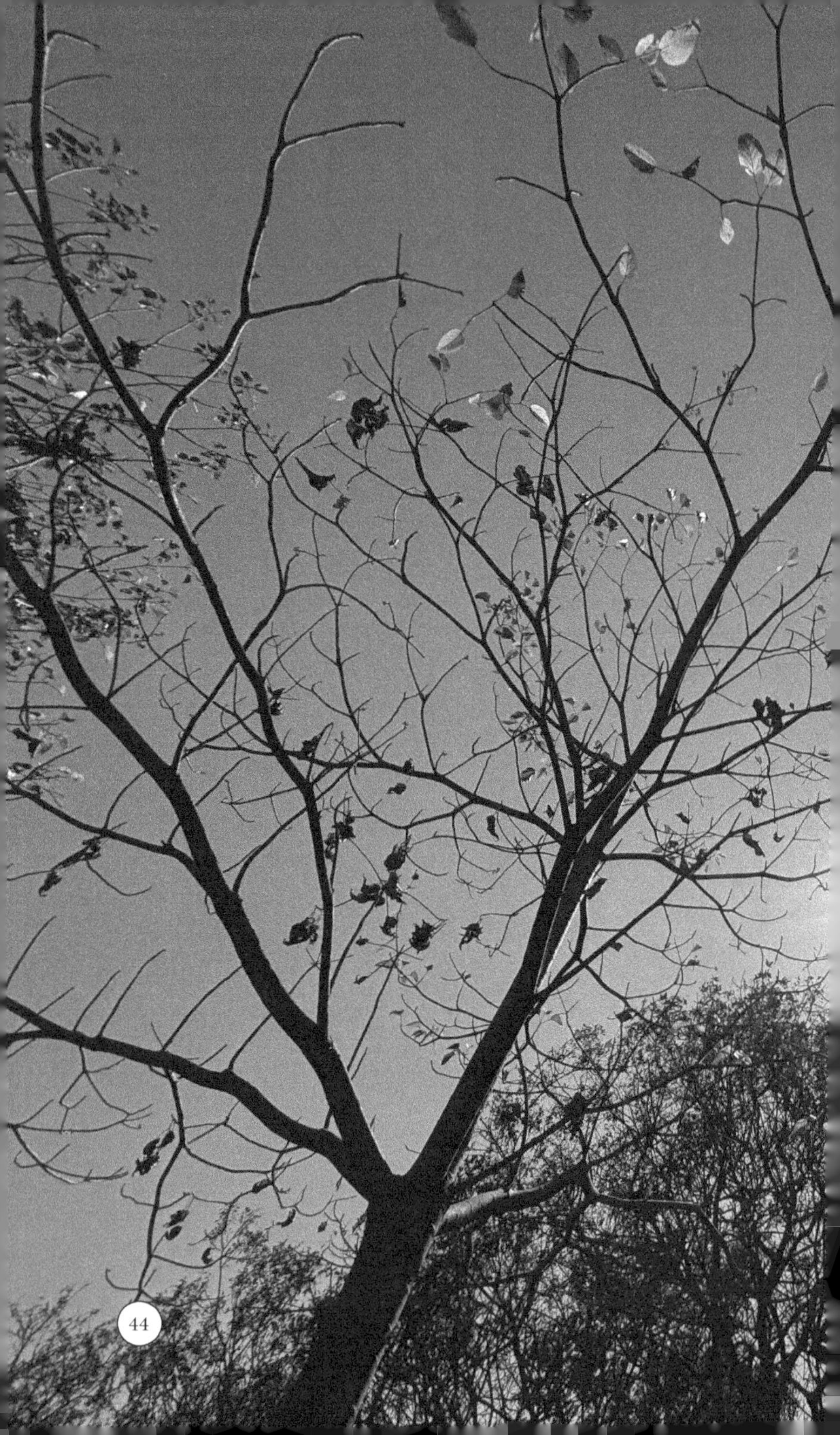

Once you name a weapon... you will be enslaved viciously.

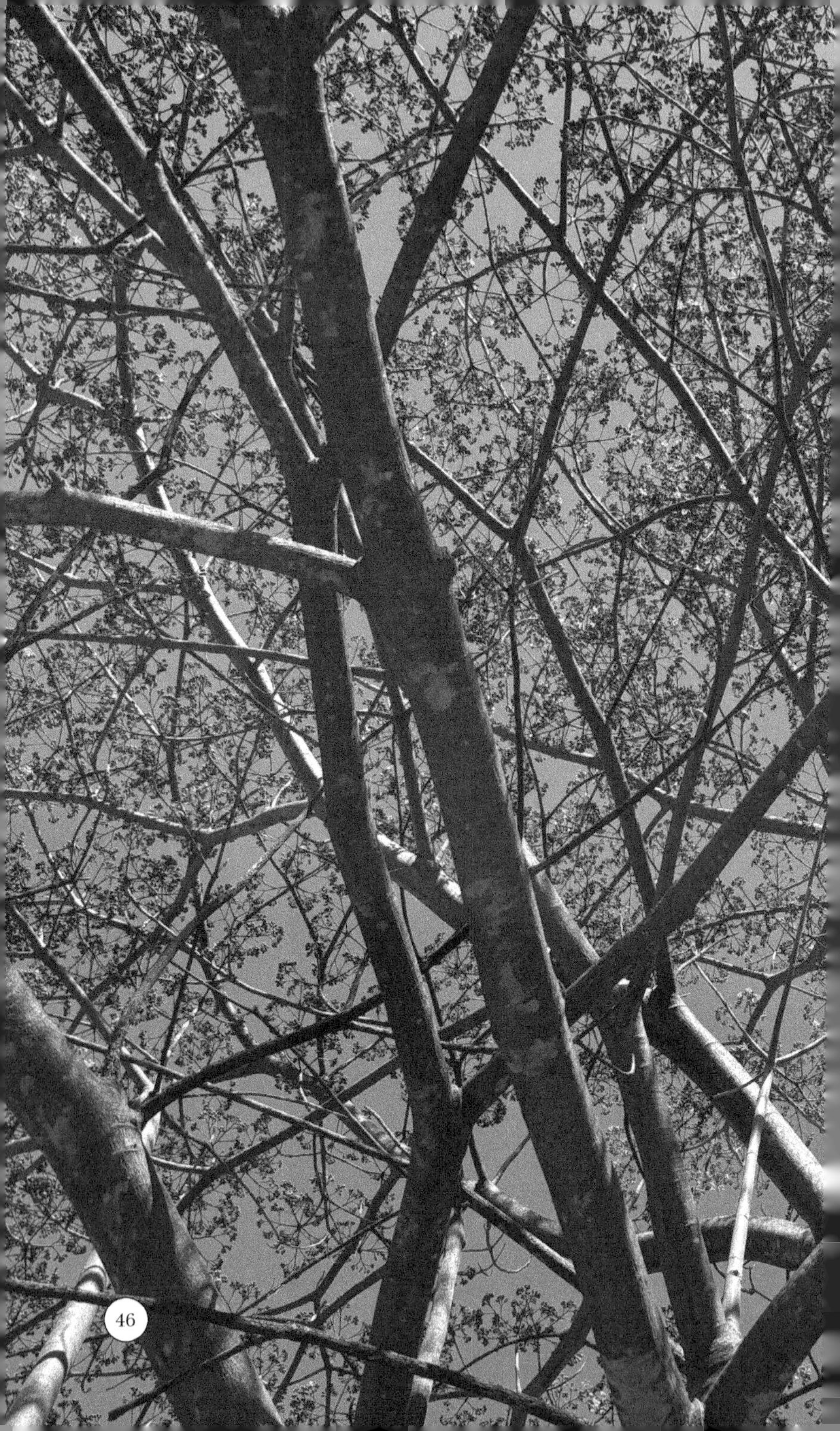

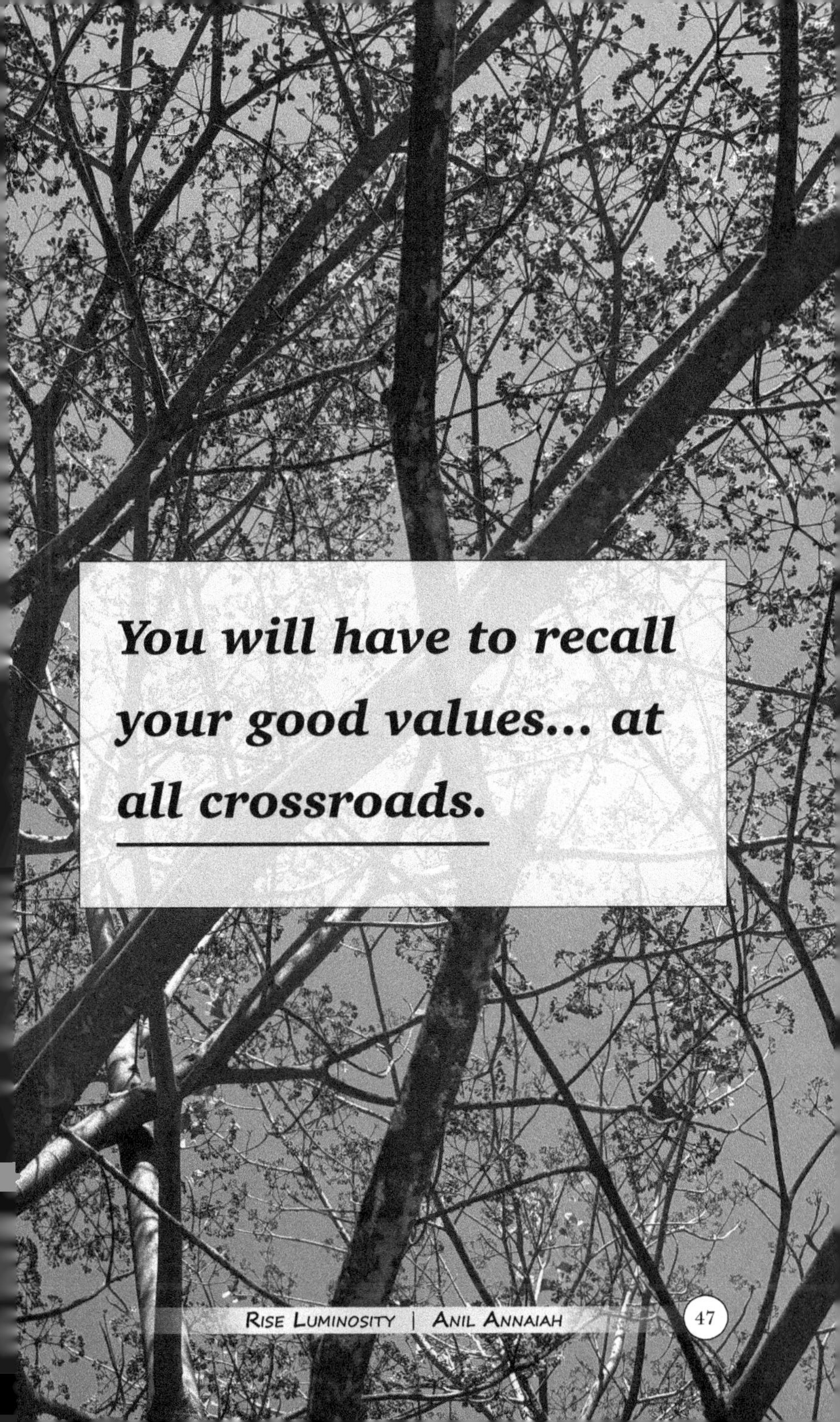

You will have to recall your good values... at all crossroads.

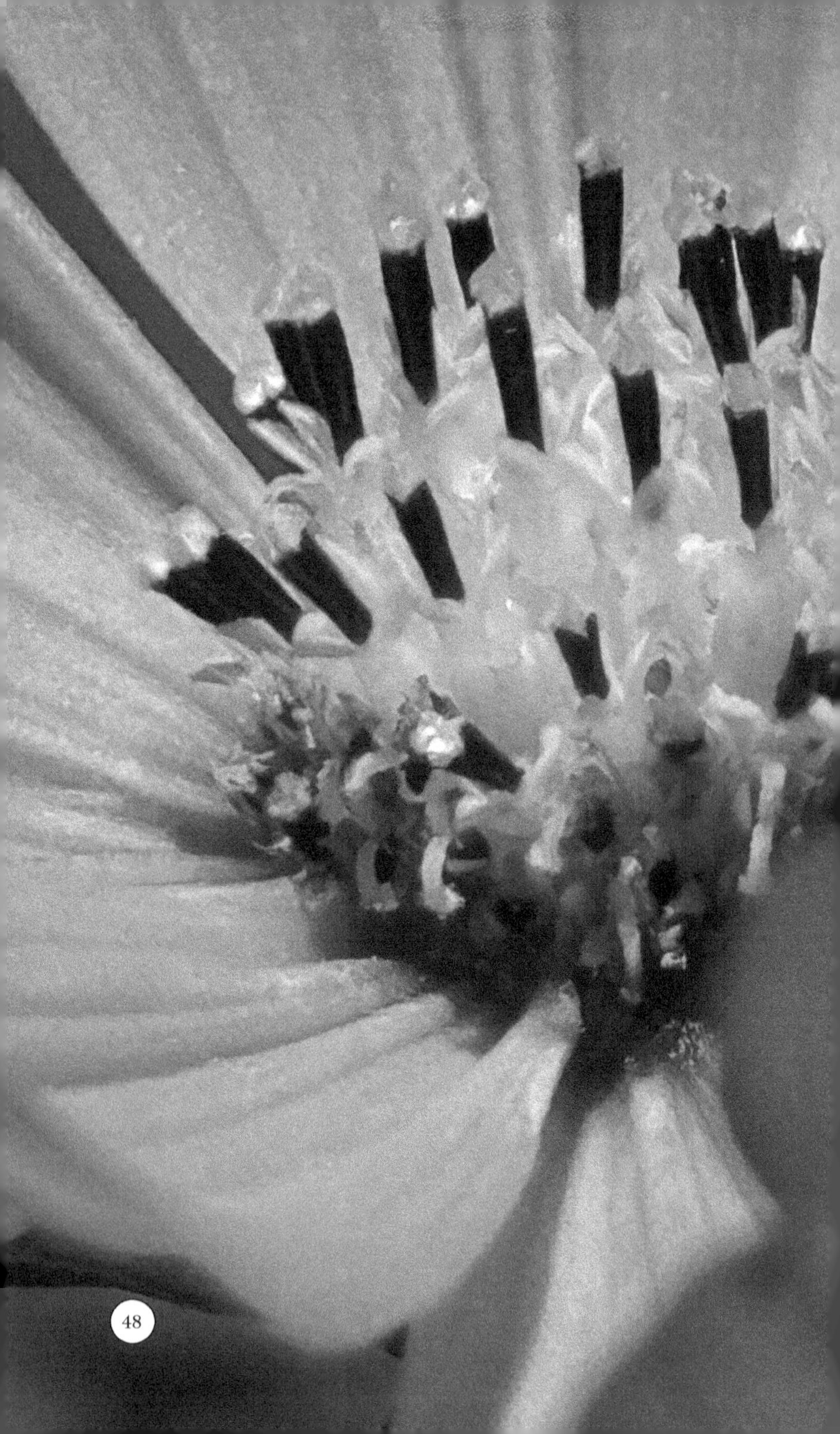

Fairweather insists...
on the use of rose
tinted glasses.

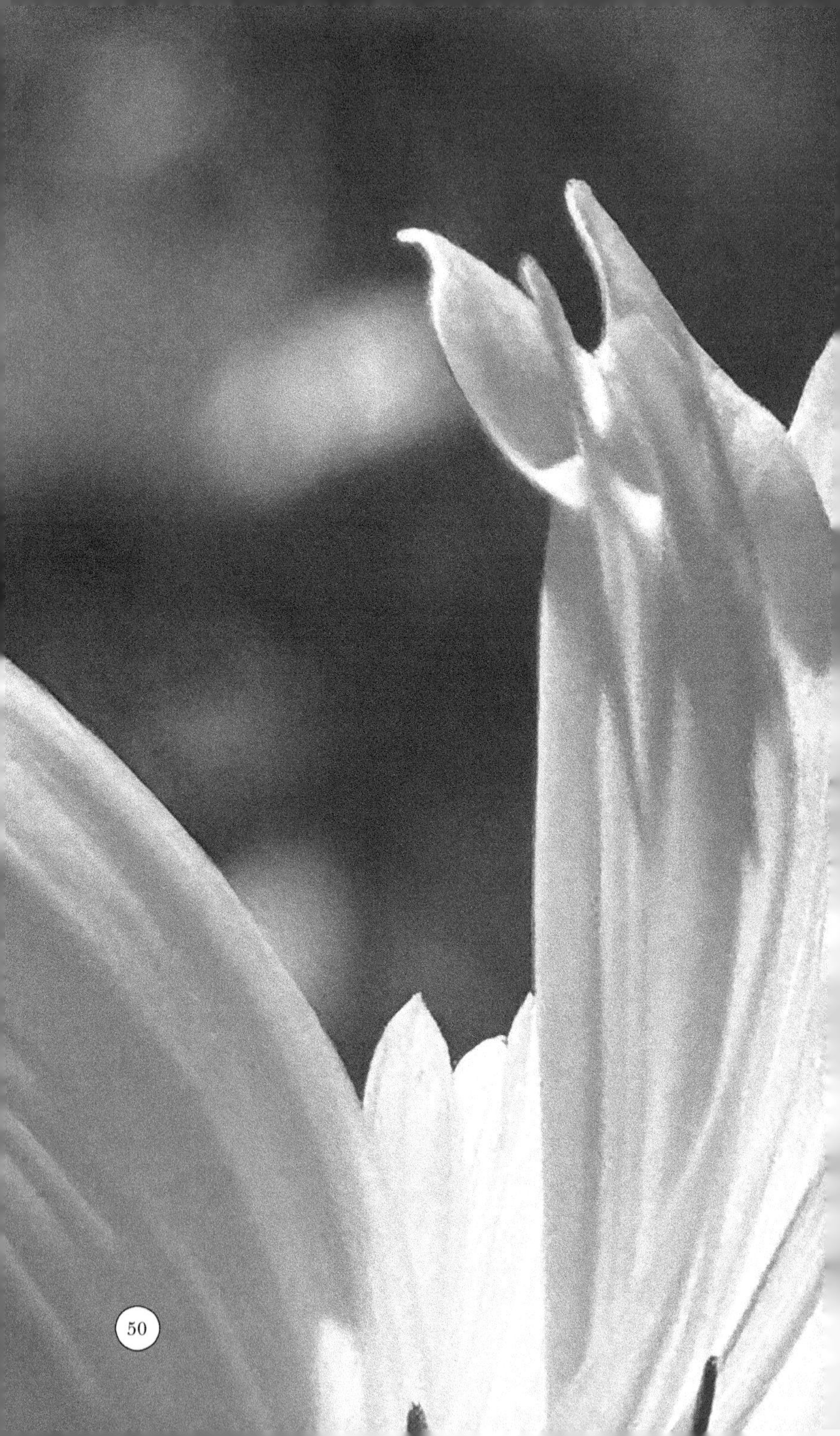

We will perish
eventually... is the
incredible strength
we carry.

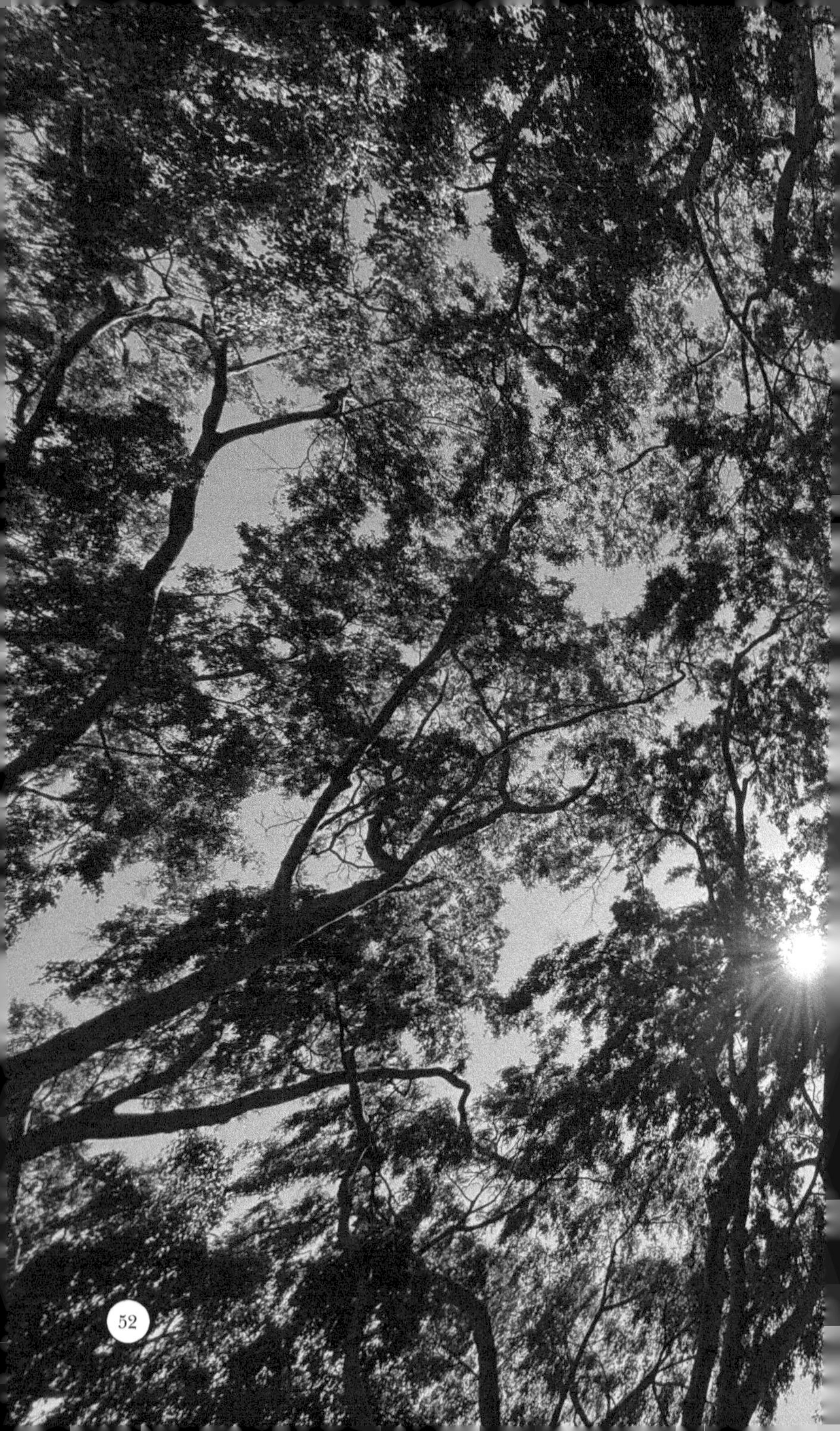

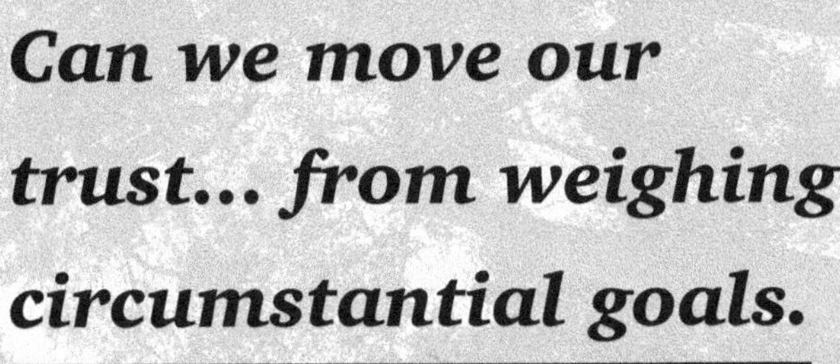
Can we move our trust... from weighing circumstantial goals.

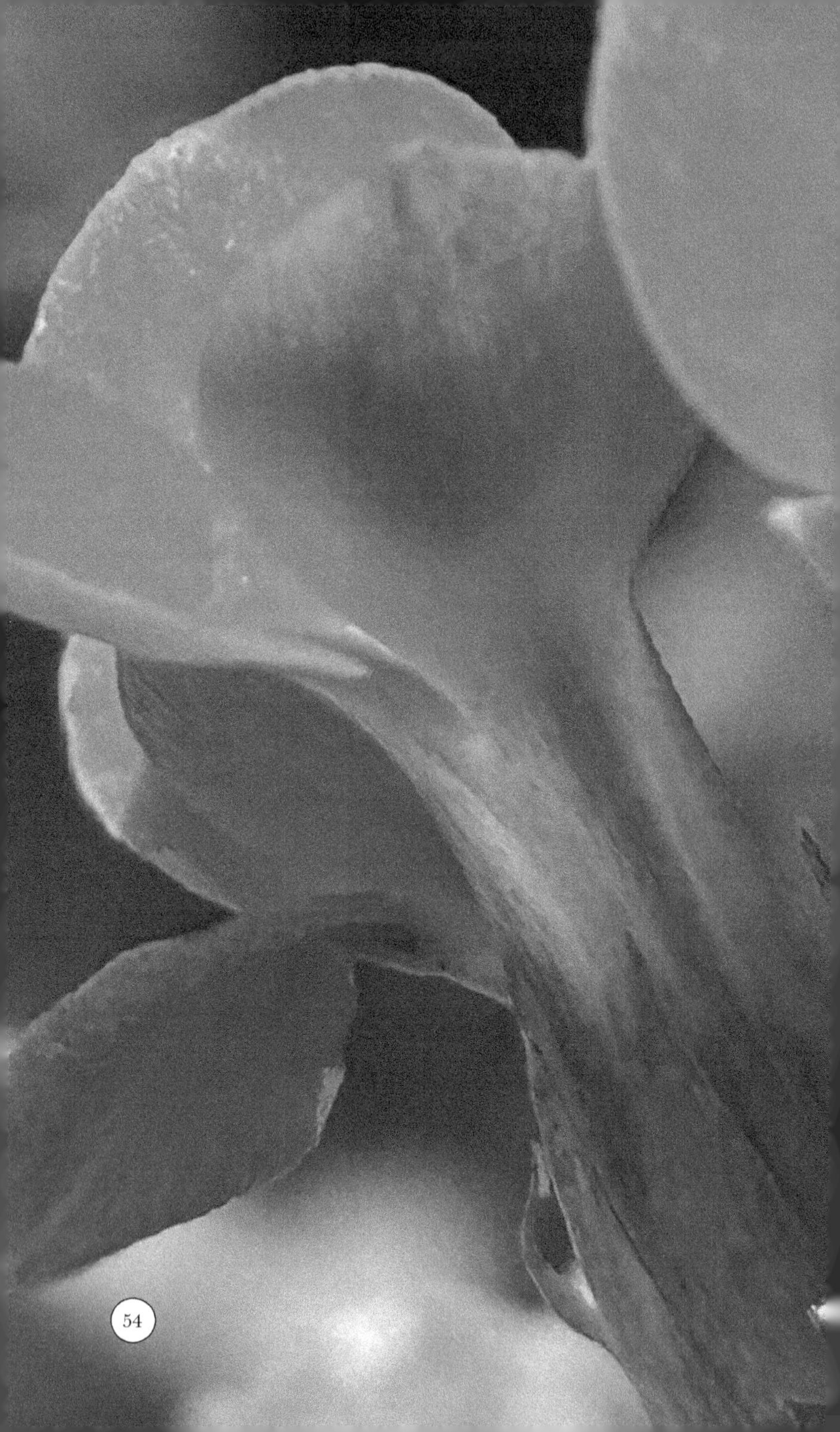

Even the thinnest of threads... can become strong enough to save you.

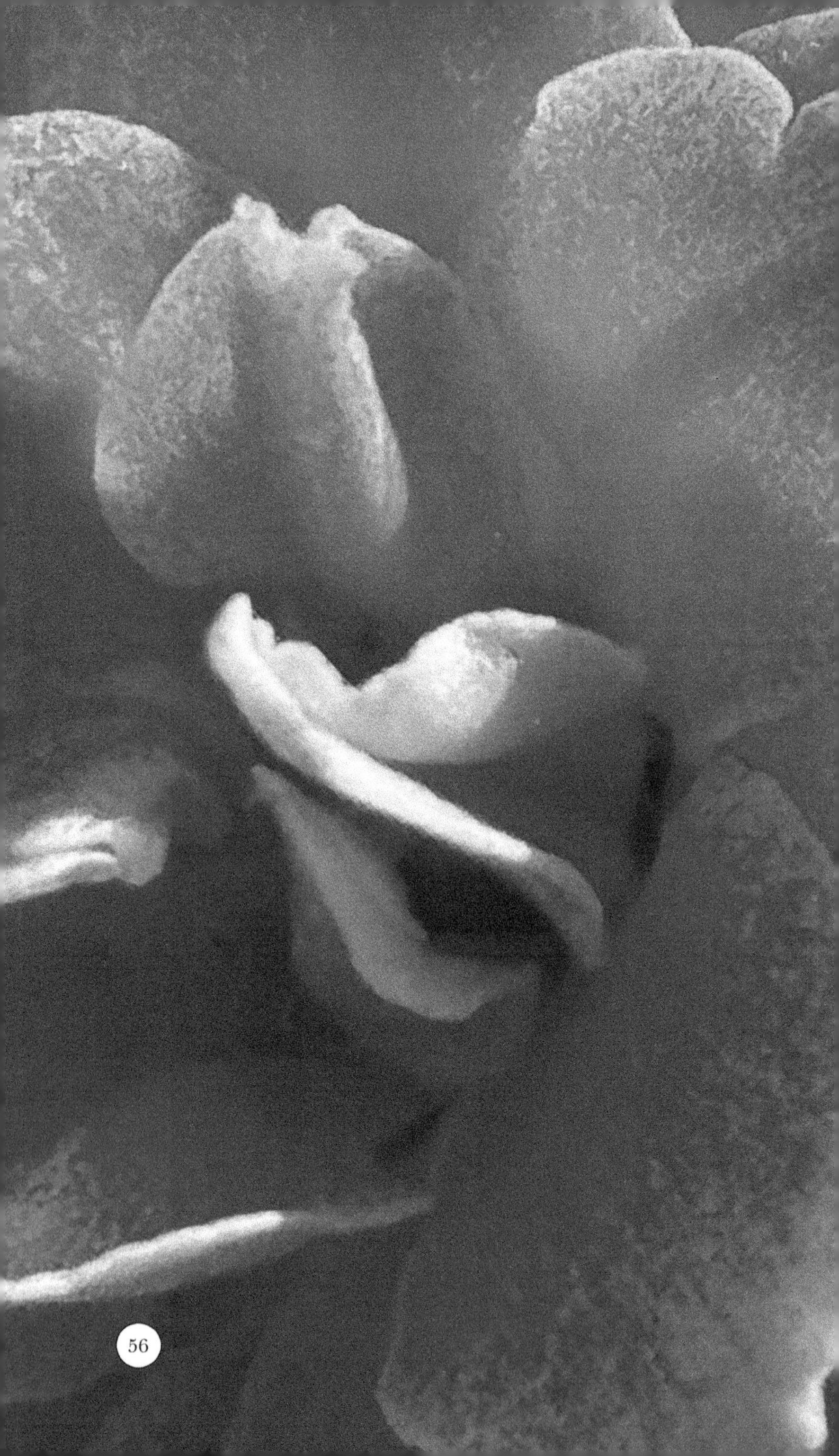

Opportunities present themselves... and missteps closely follow.

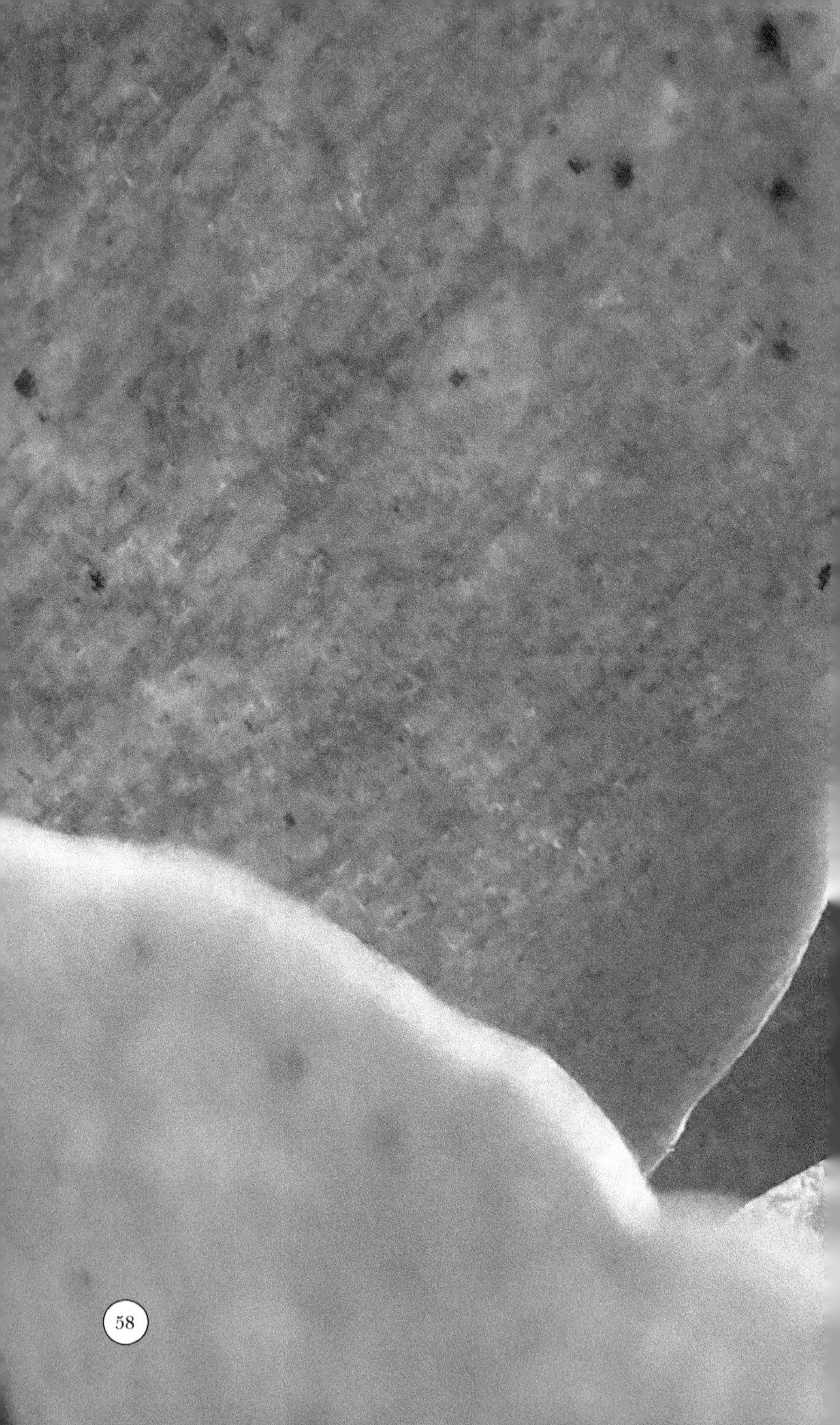

Why do we care to serve Joy better... than the sorrow.

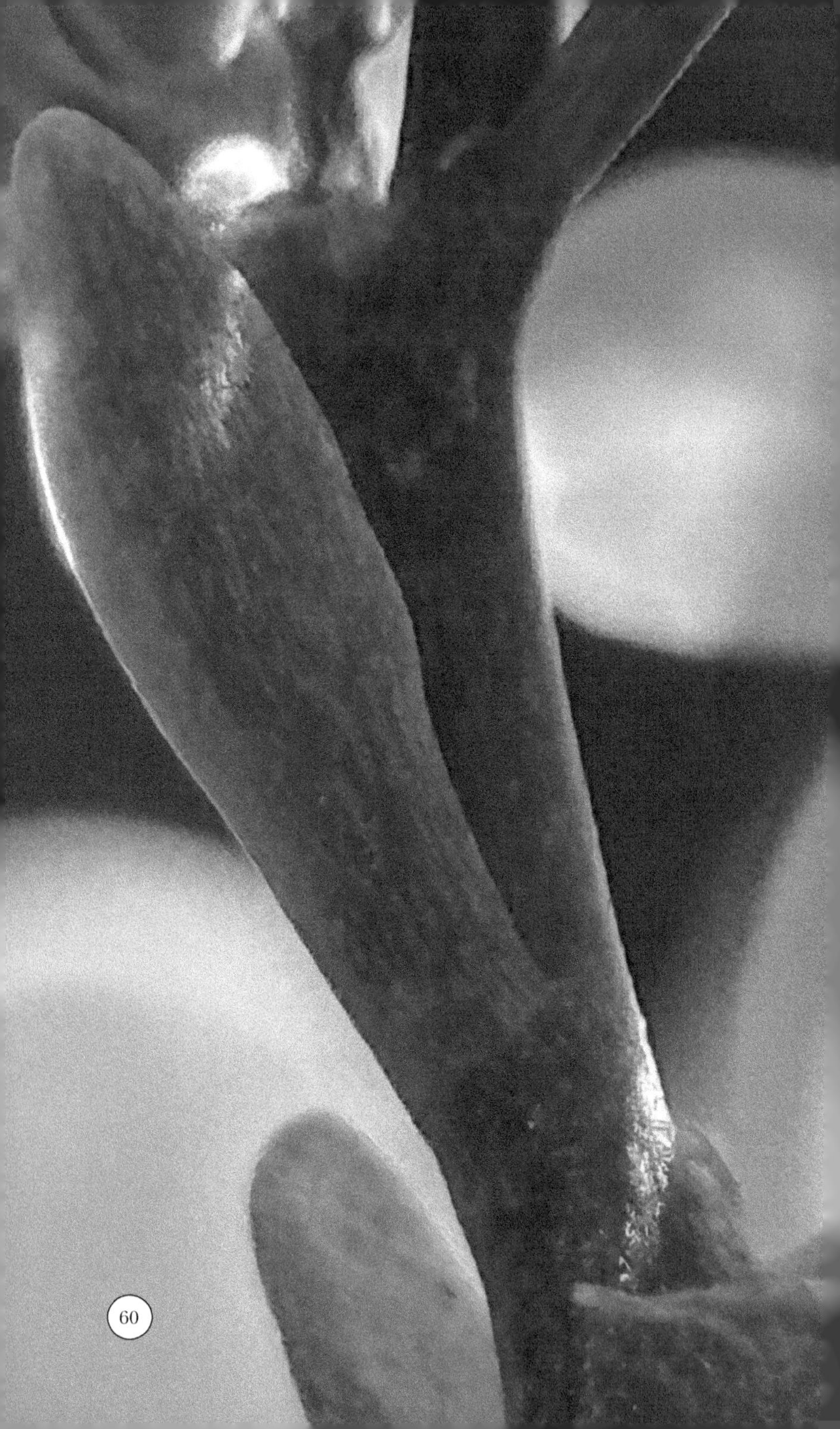

**Your inner light...
needs your trust and
friendship.**

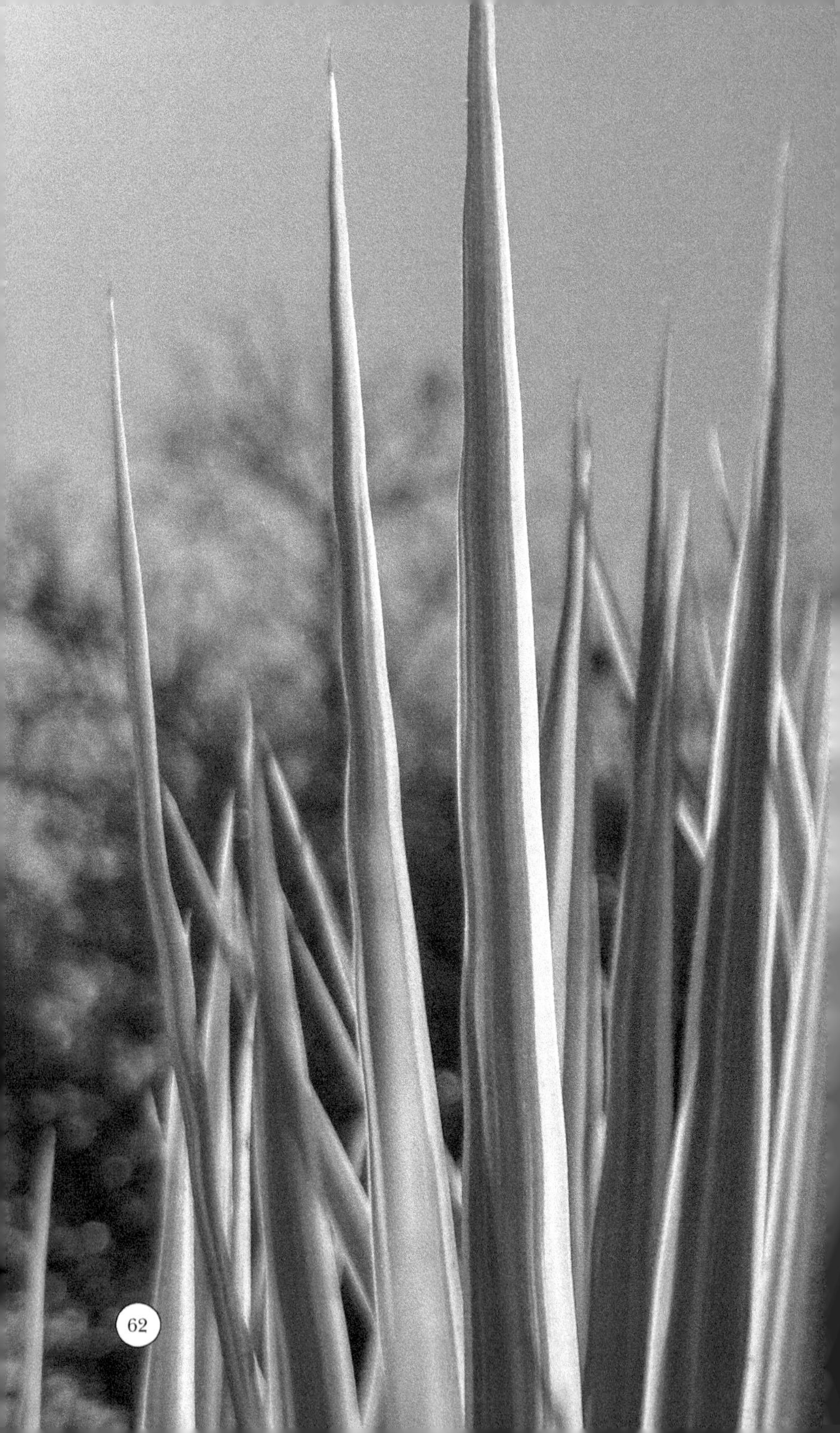

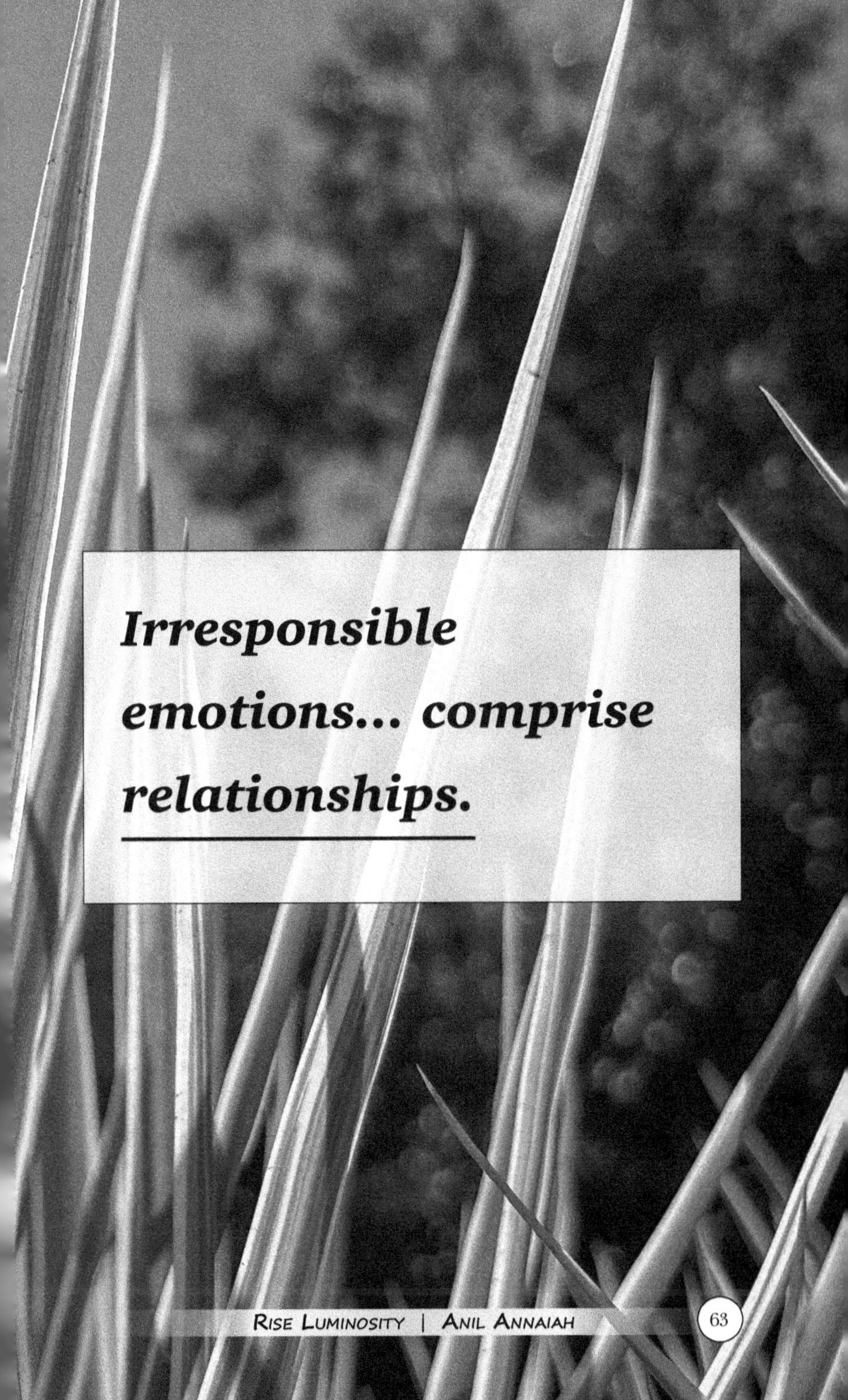

Irresponsible emotions... comprise relationships.

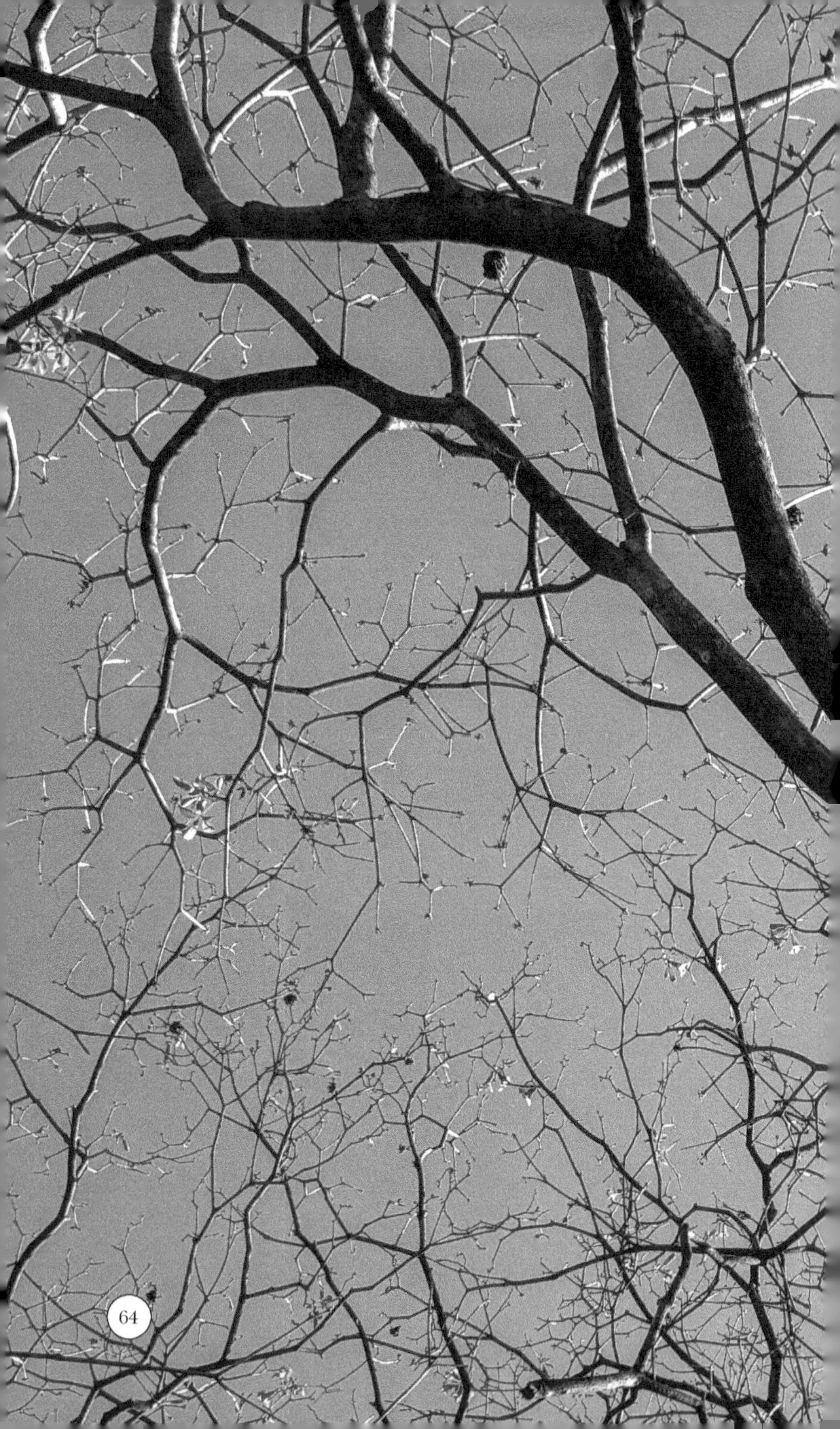

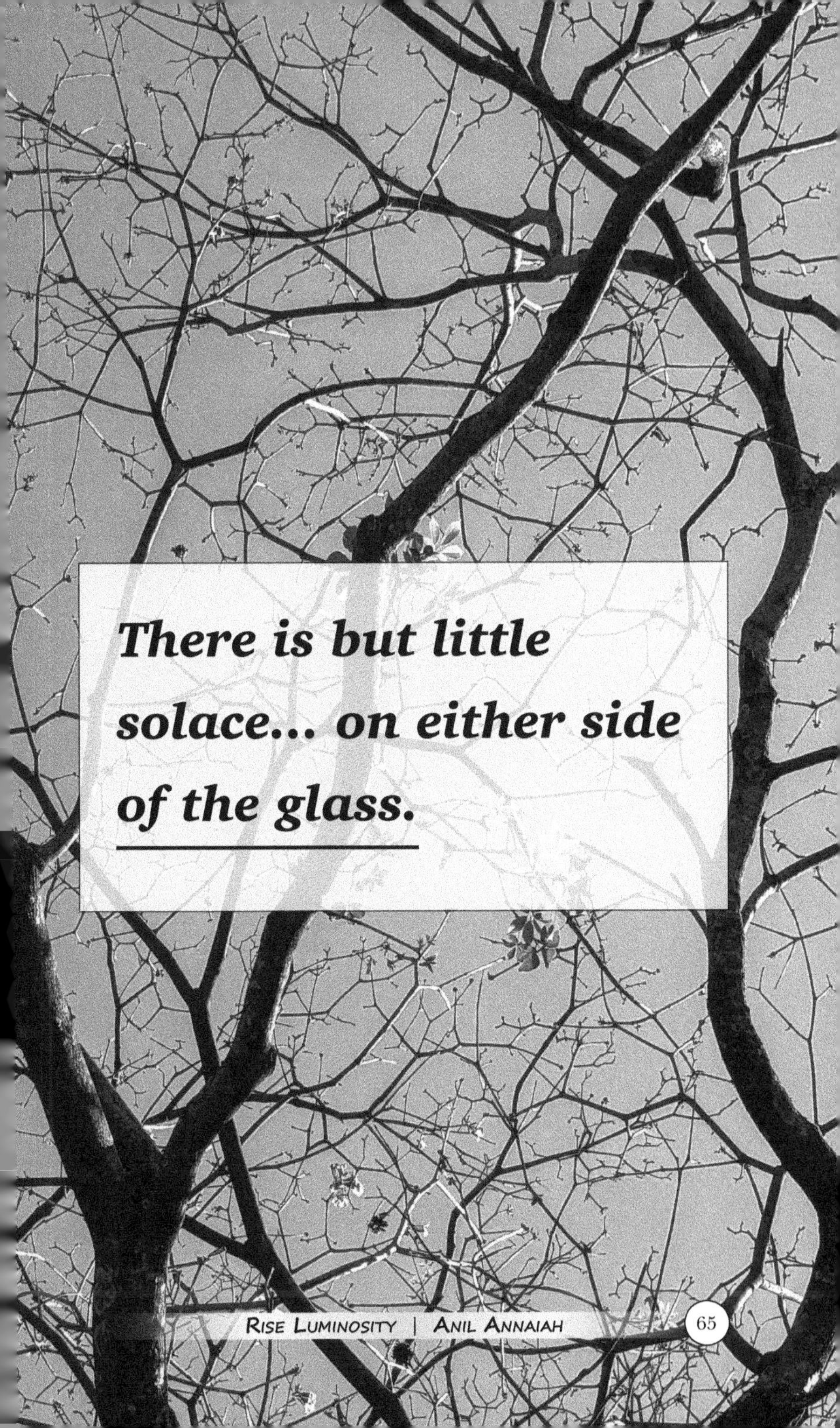

There is but little solace... on either side of the glass.

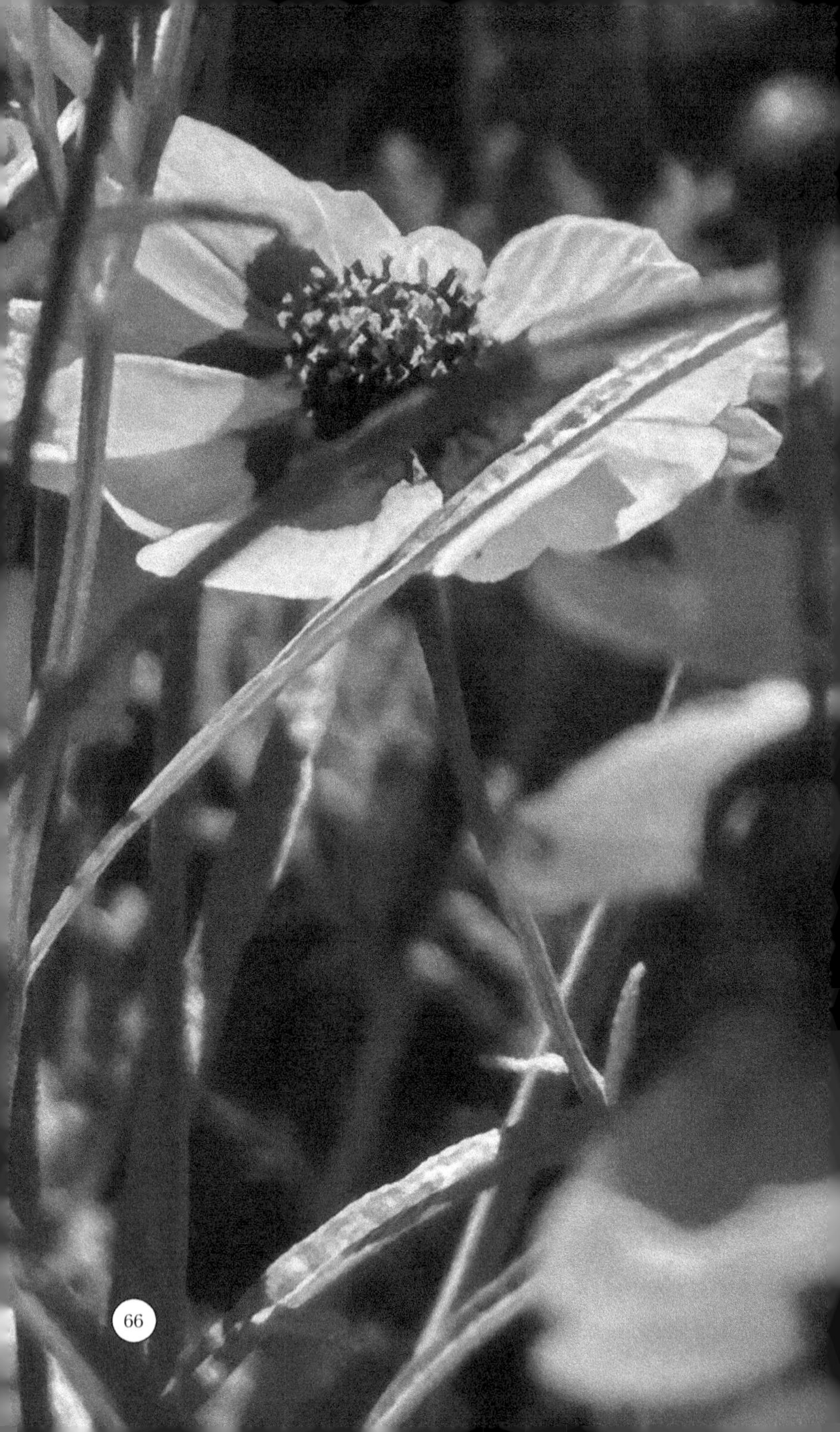

Stopping or stepping out sometimes from your path... is not inevitable.

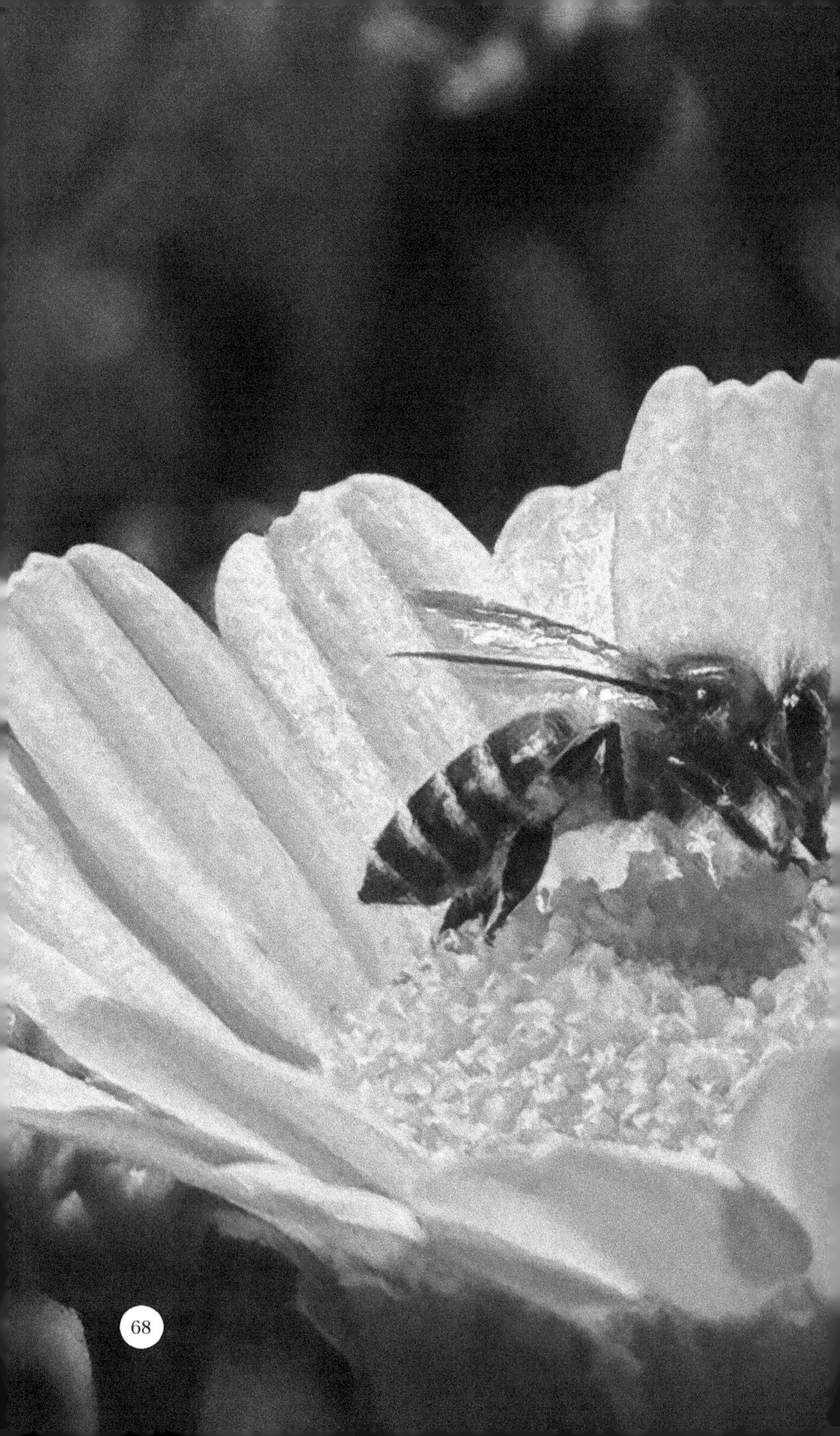

We constantly propel ourselves... to meet insignificant ends.

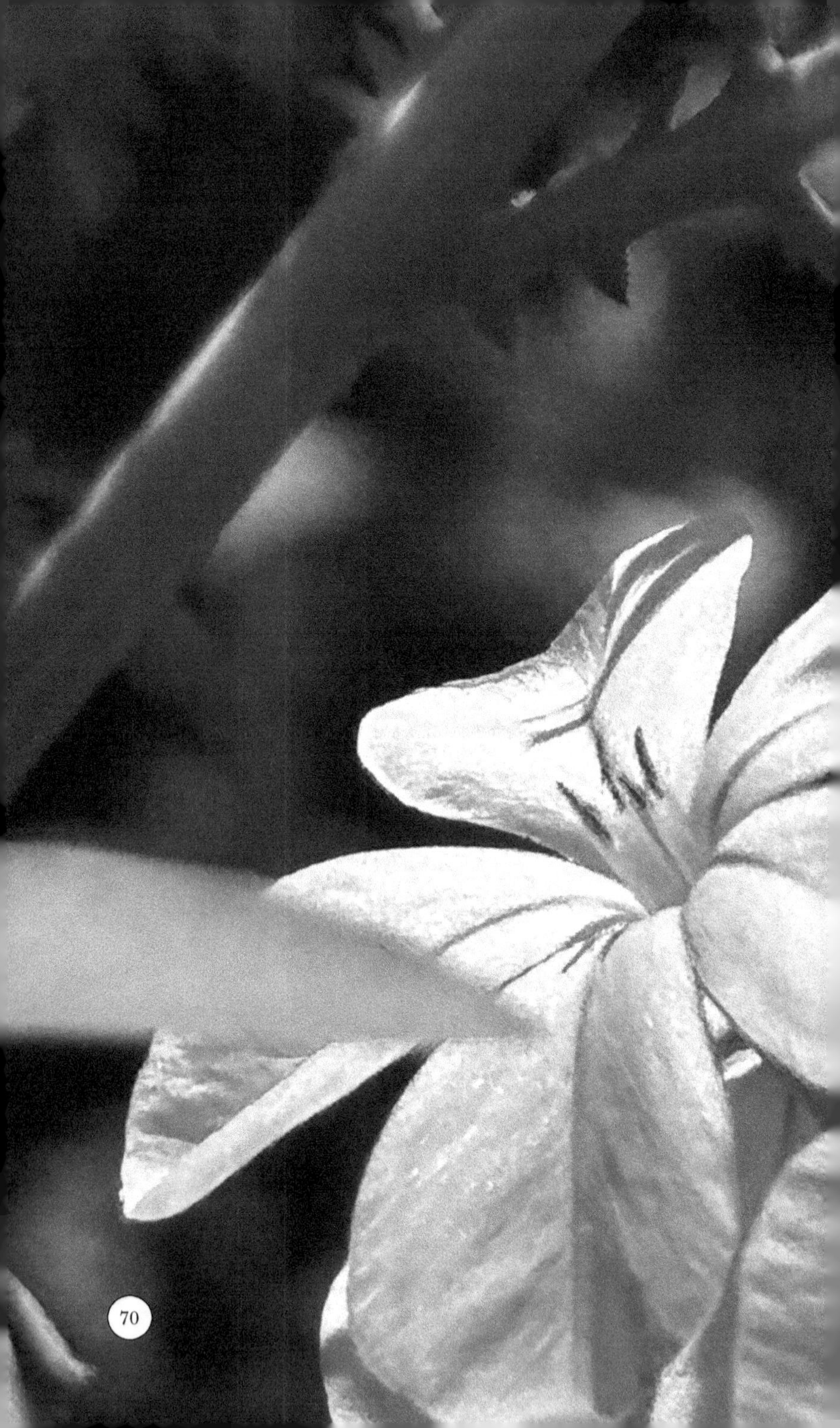

*Our worst punishment...
invariably comes from
our ego.*

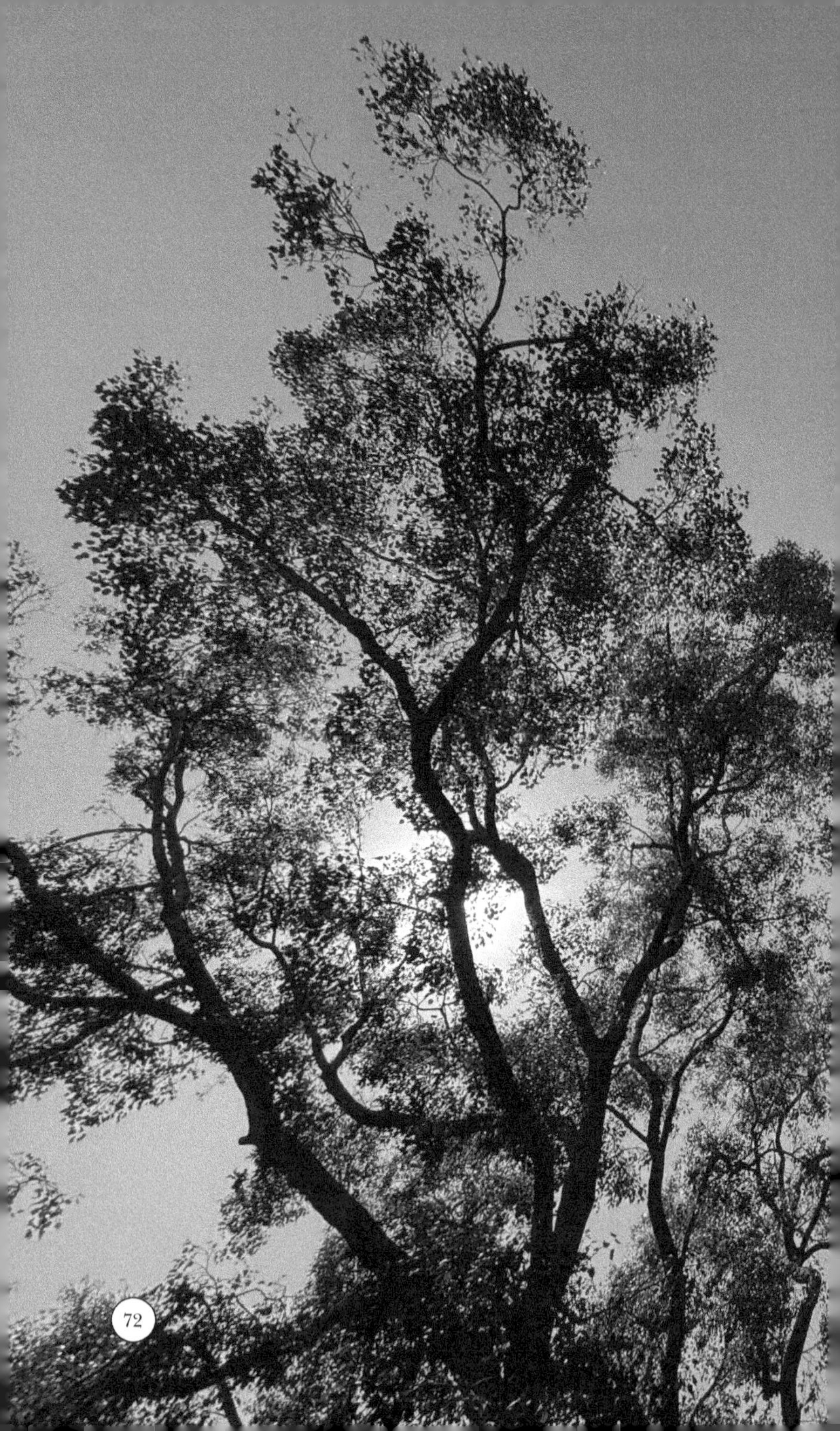

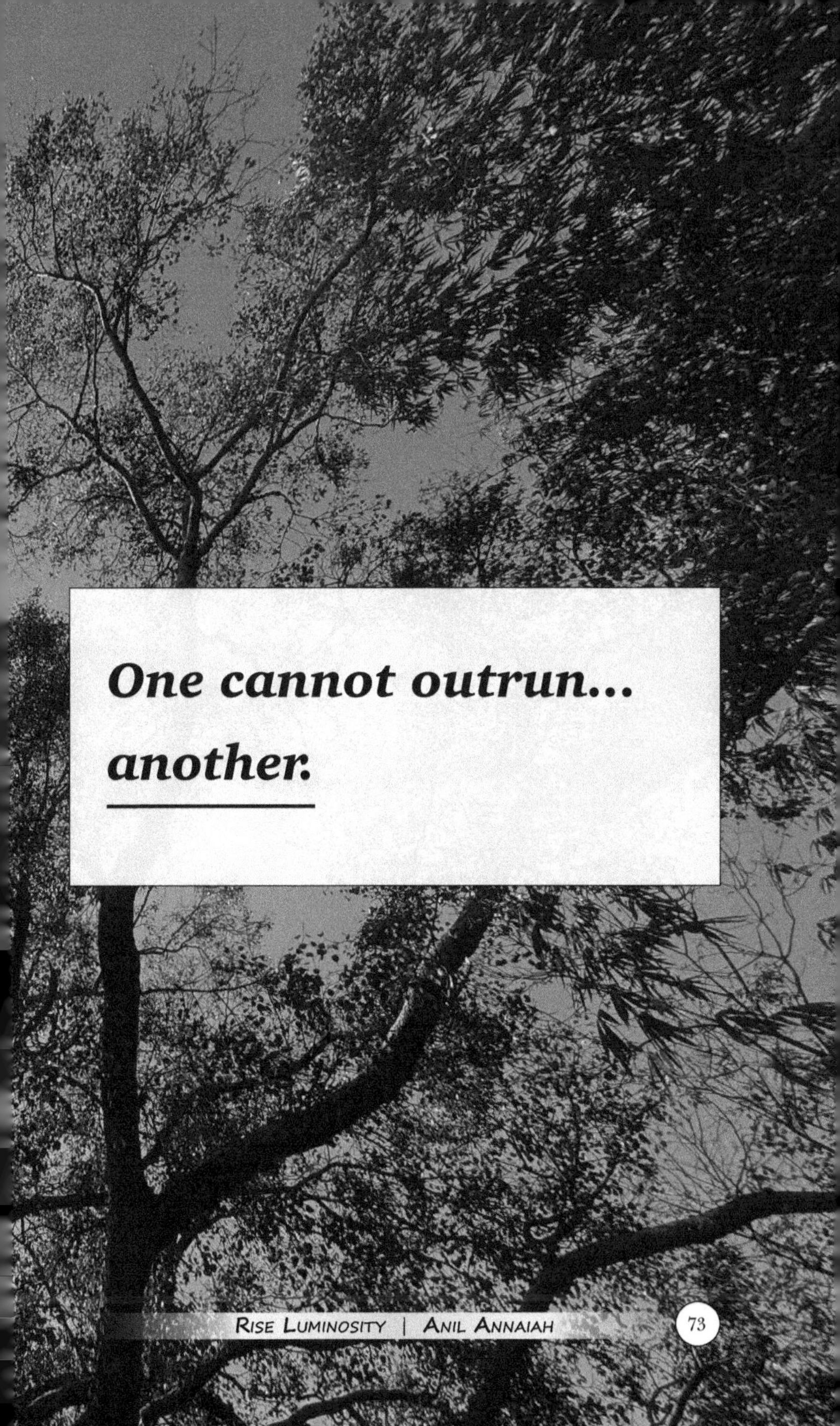

One cannot outrun...
another.

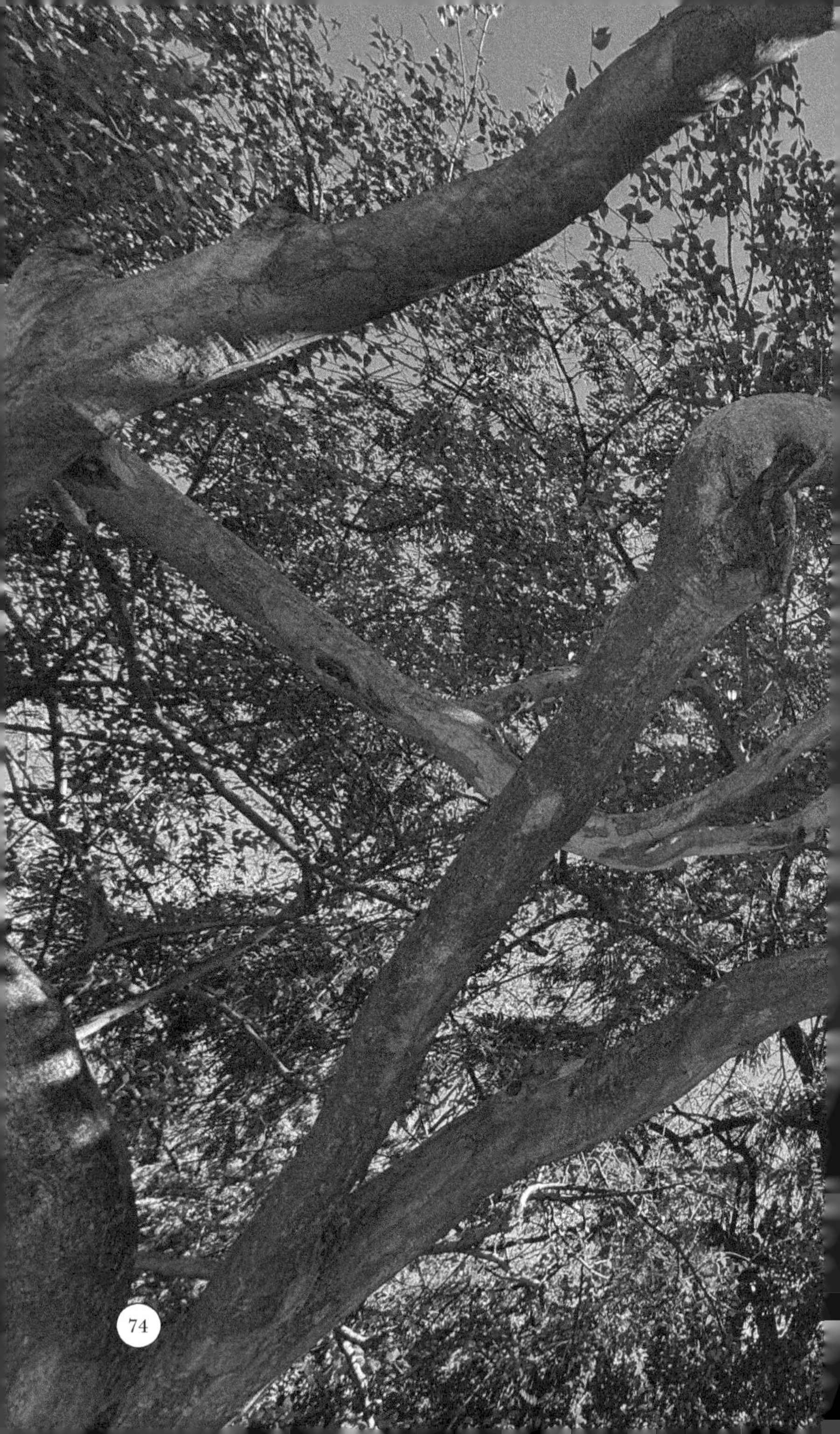

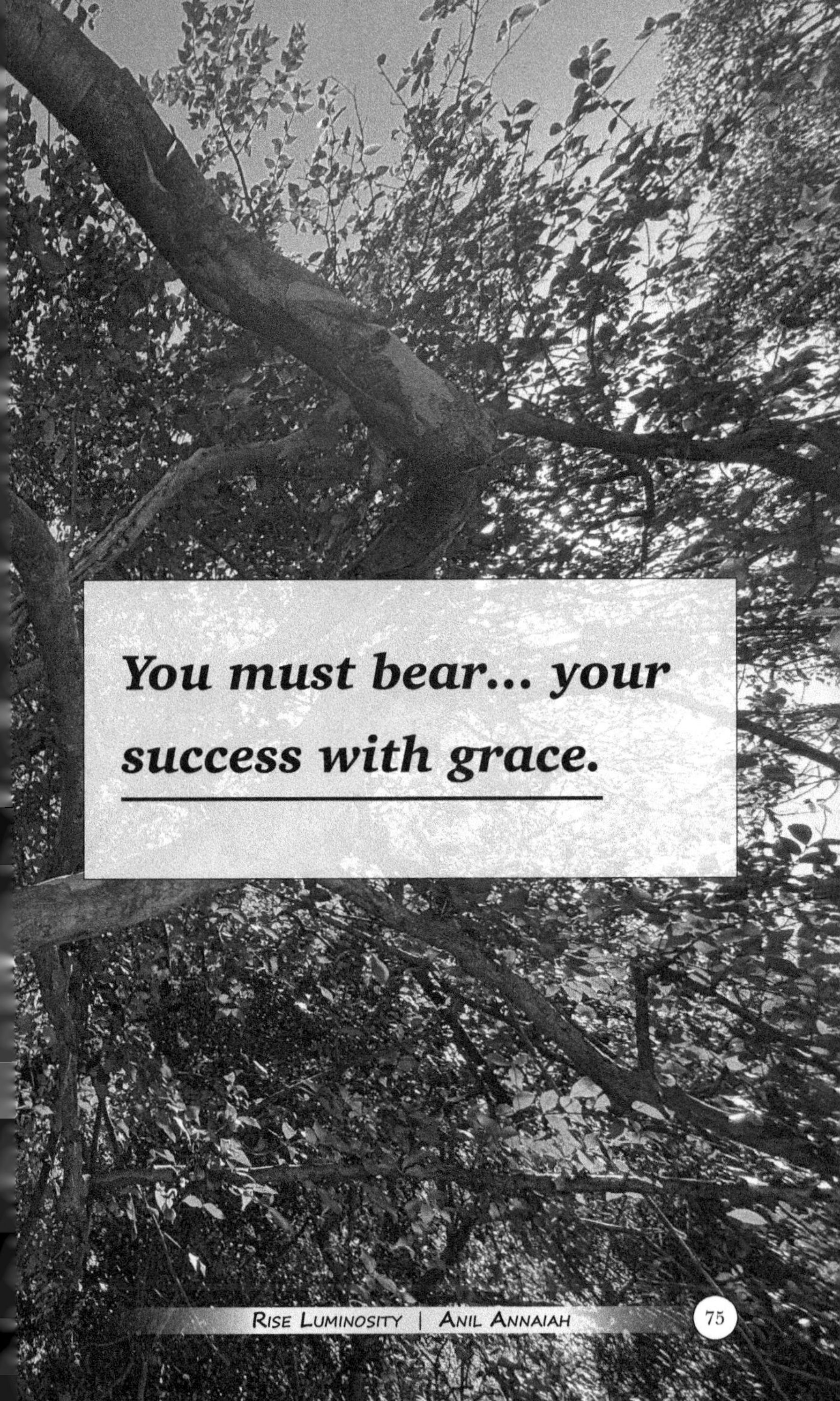

You must bear... your success with grace.

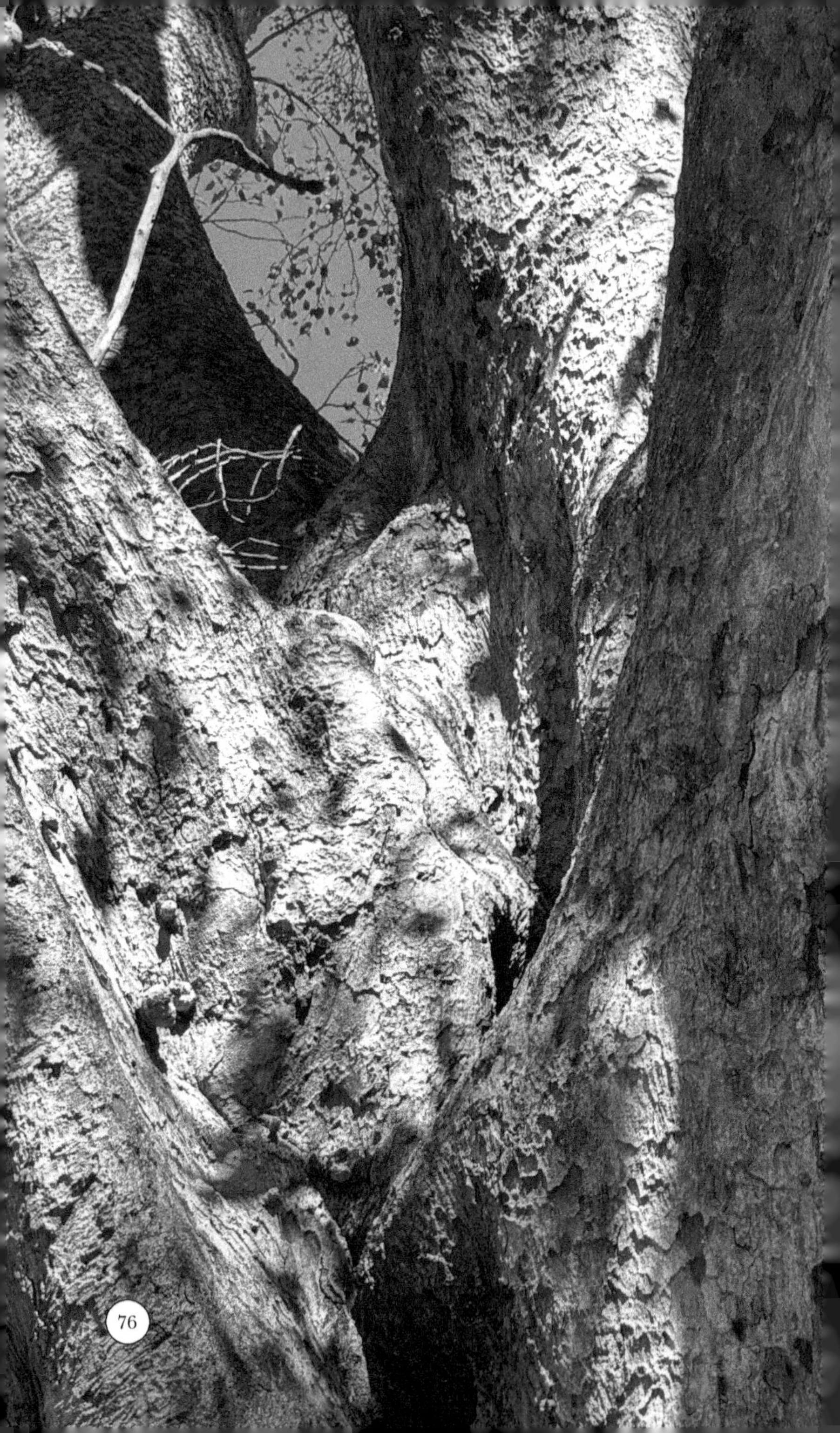

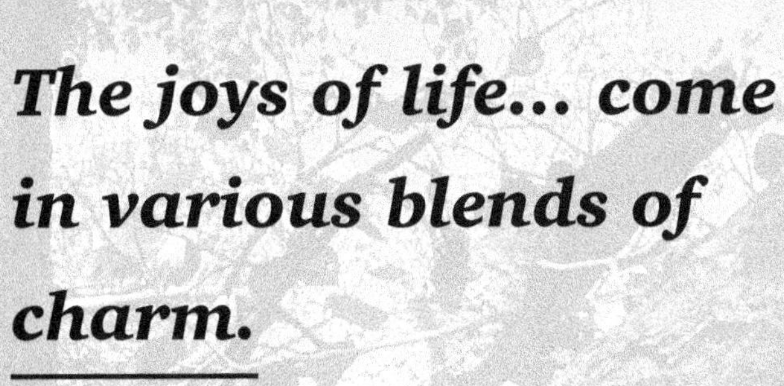

The joys of life... come in various blends of charm.

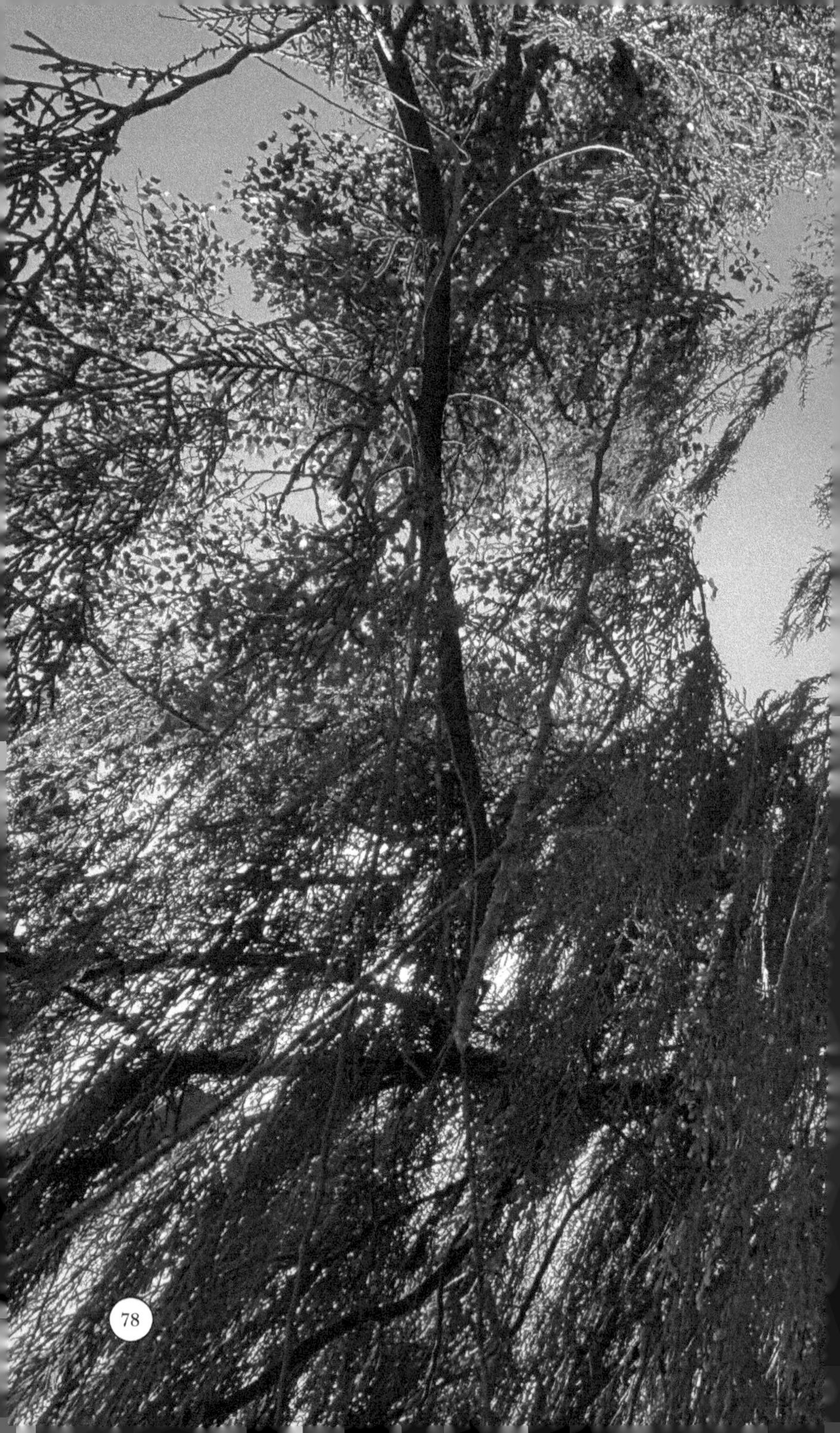

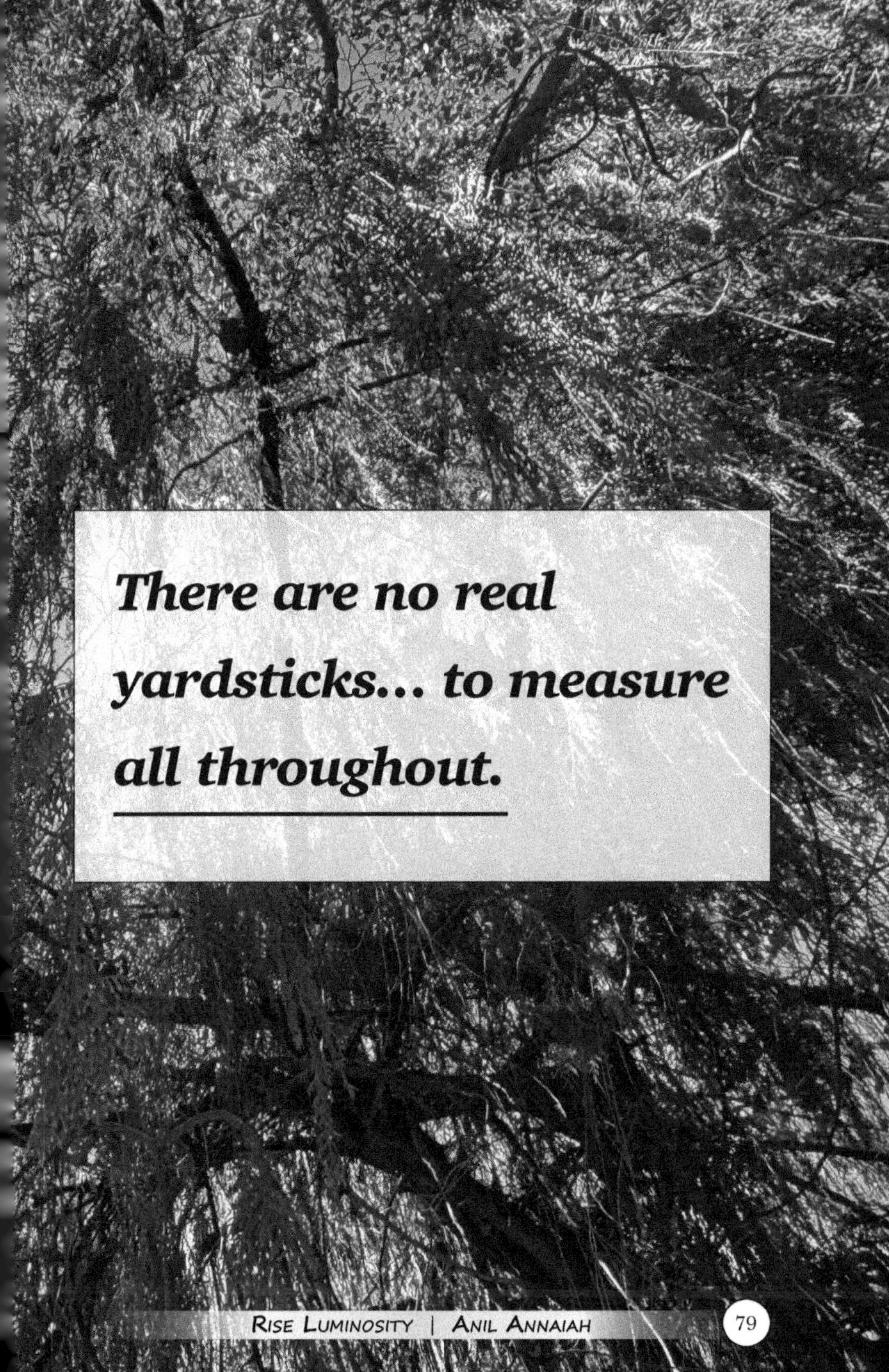

There are no real yardsticks... to measure all throughout.

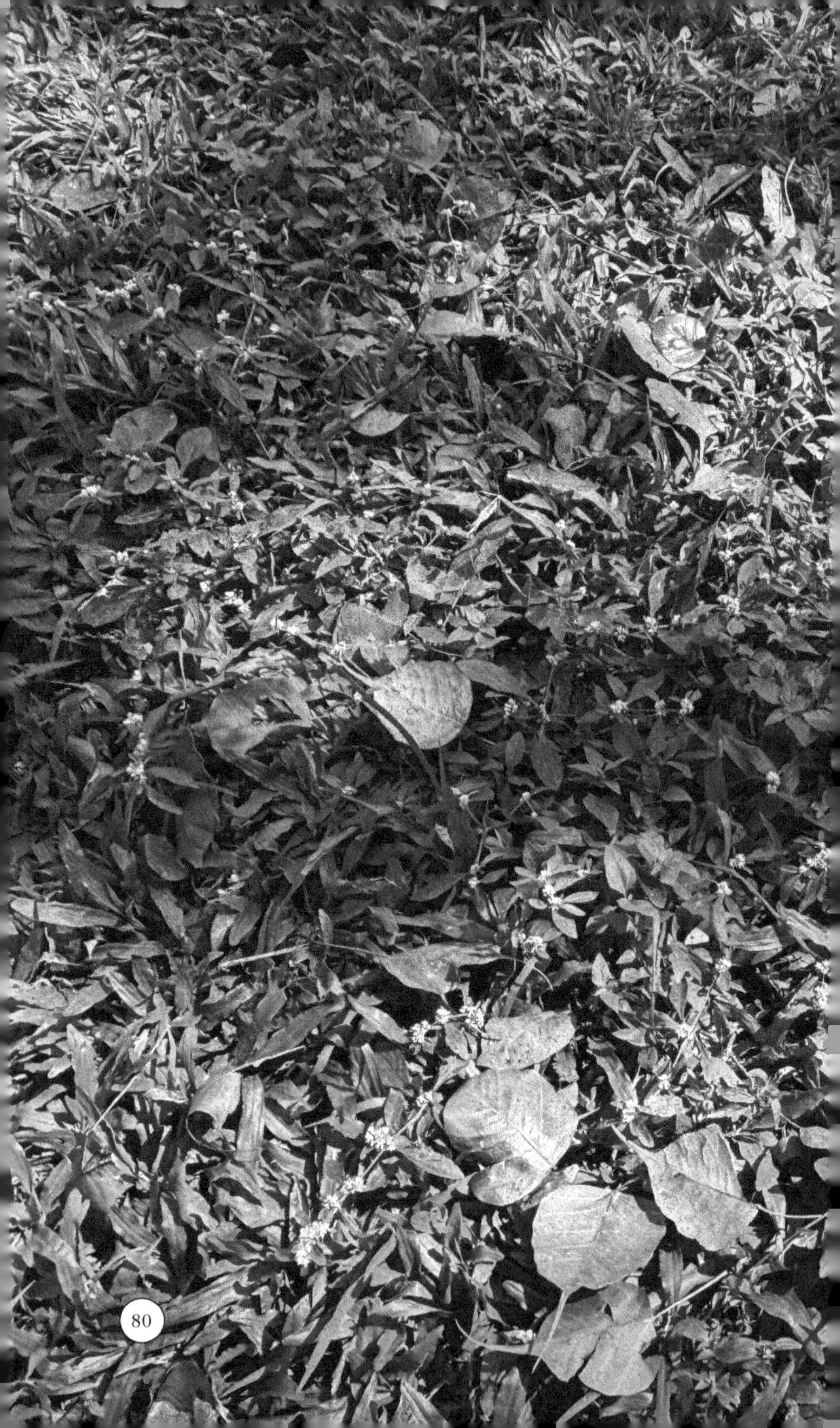

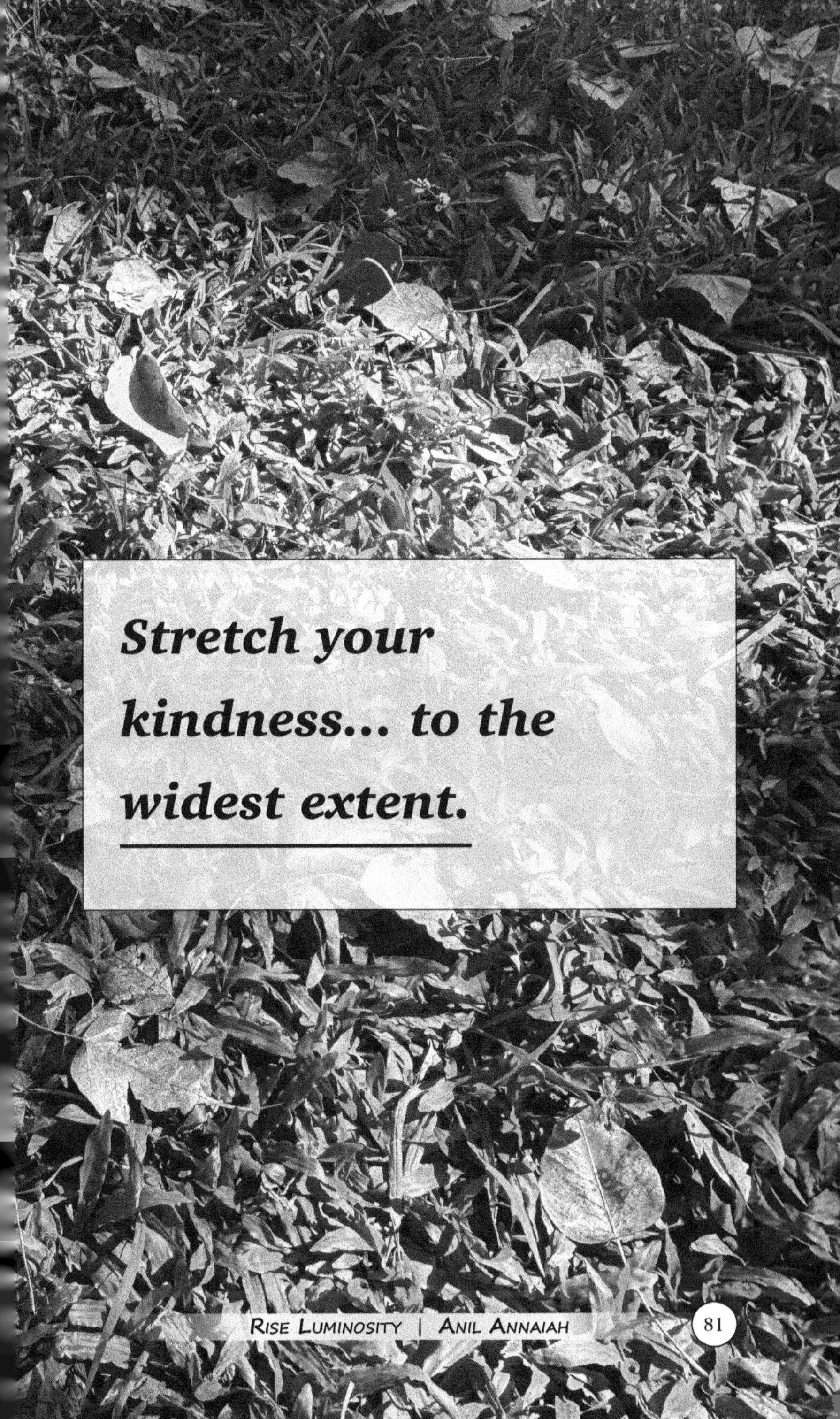
Stretch your kindness... to the widest extent.

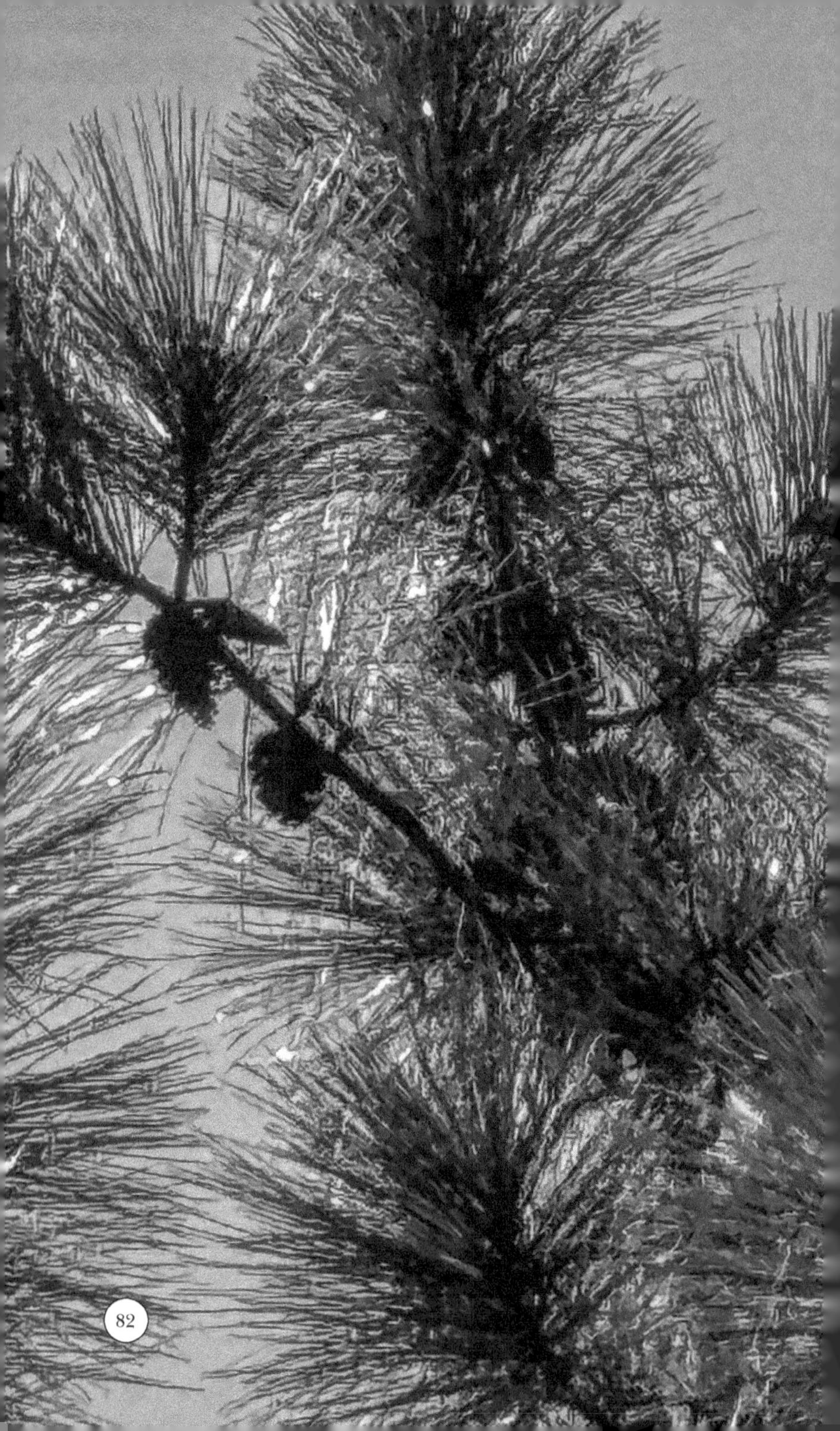

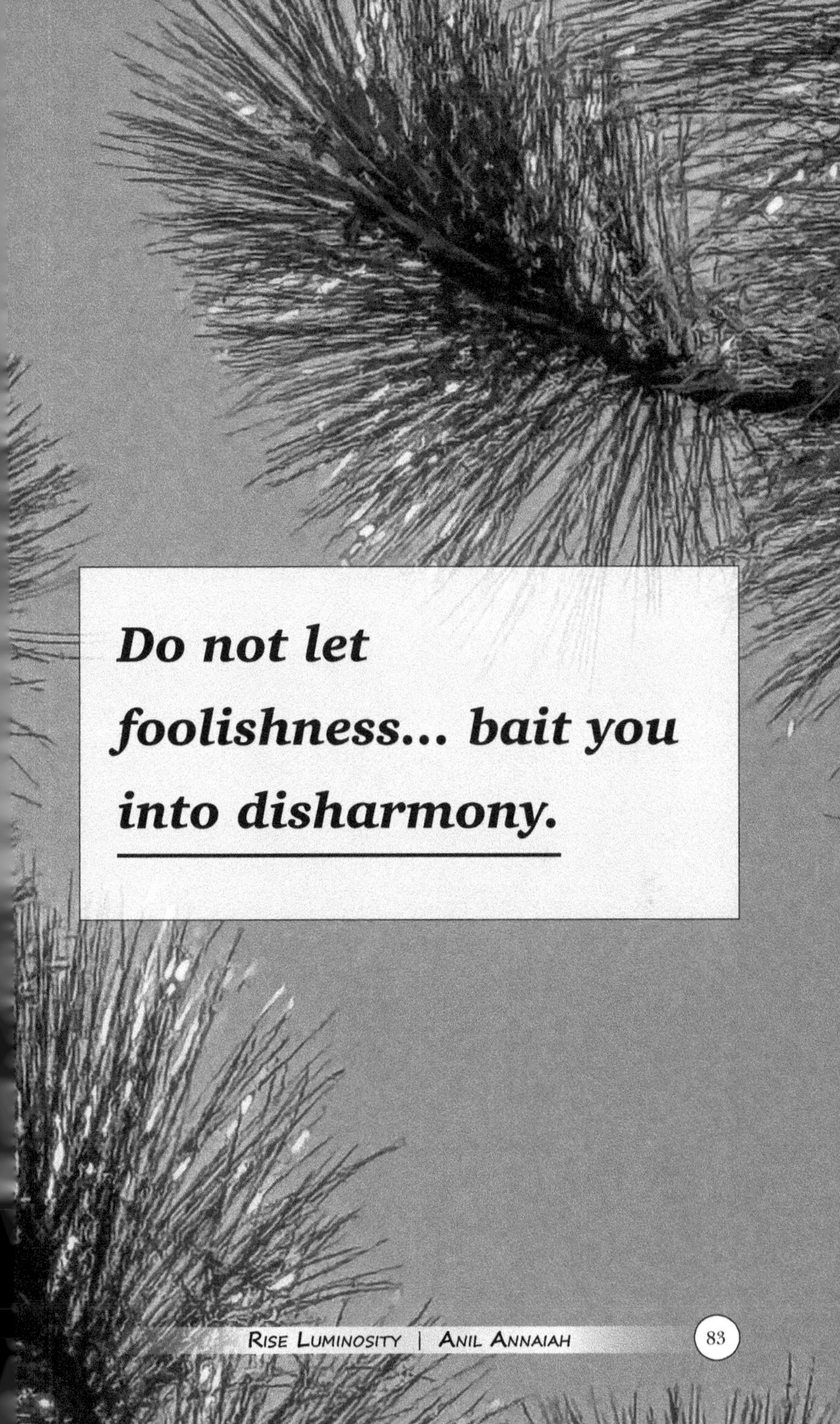
Do not let
foolishness... bait you
into disharmony.

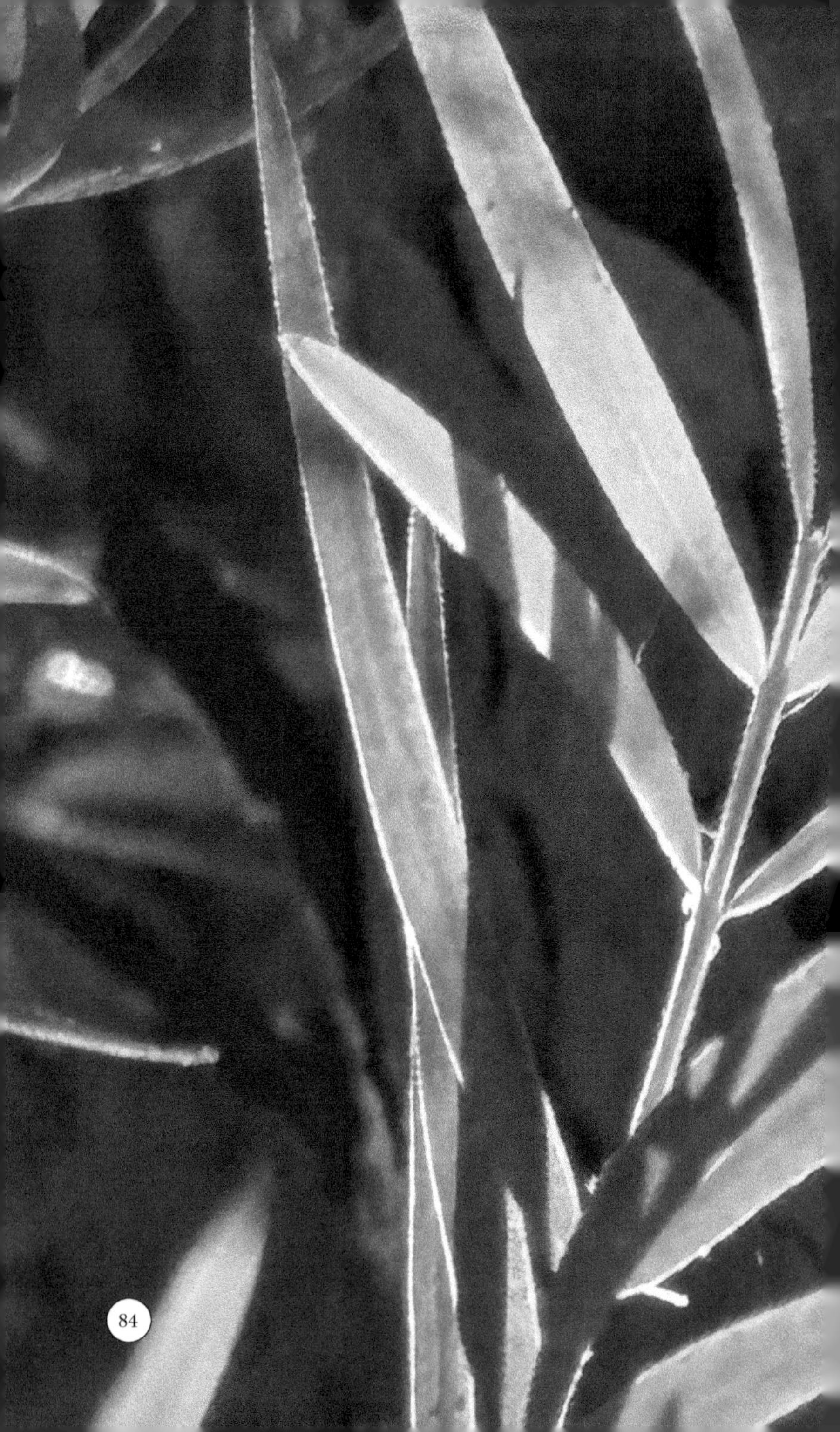

Only with gentle moderation... will we not fall into chaos.

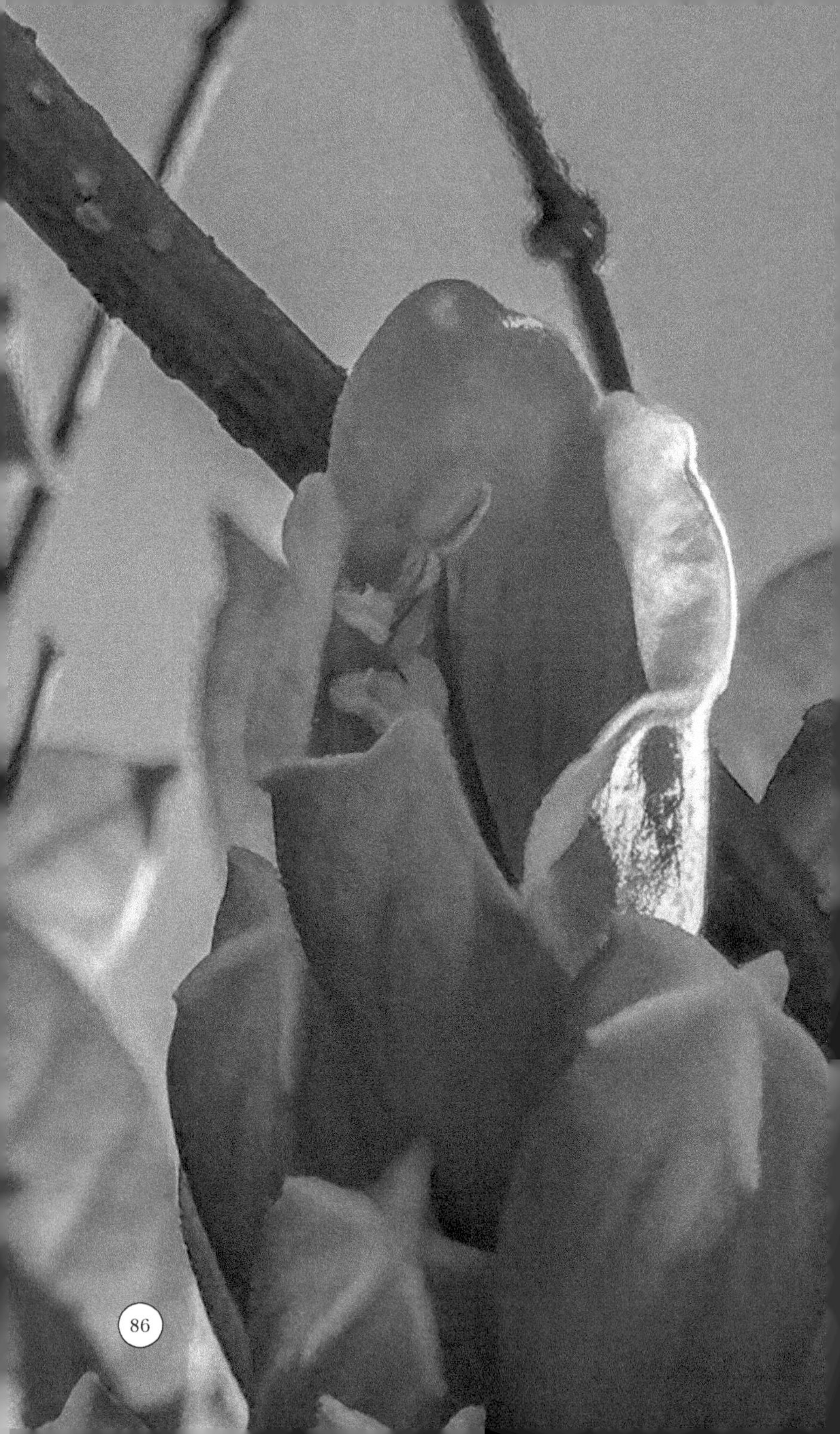

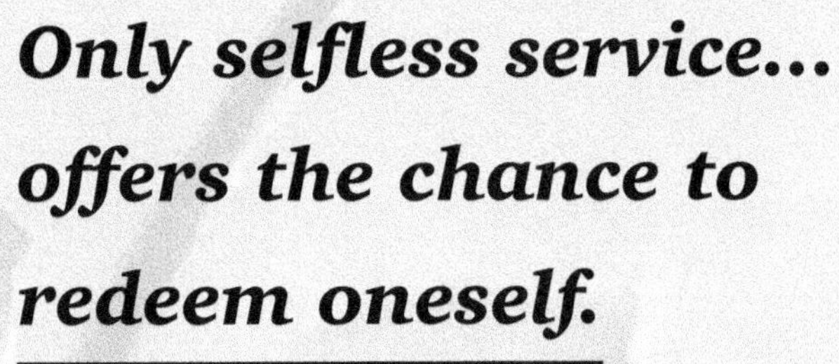

Only selfless service...
offers the chance to
redeem oneself.

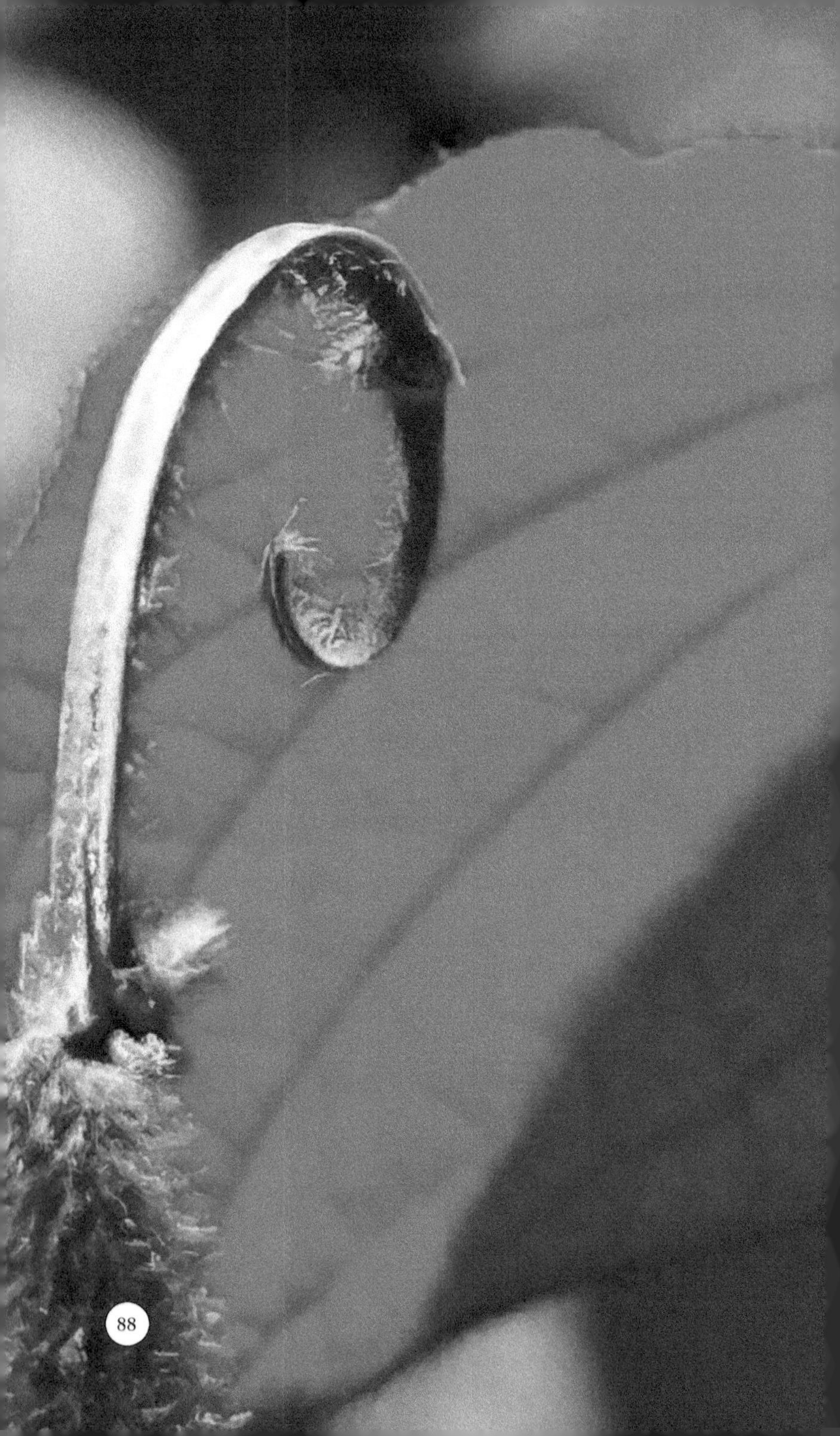

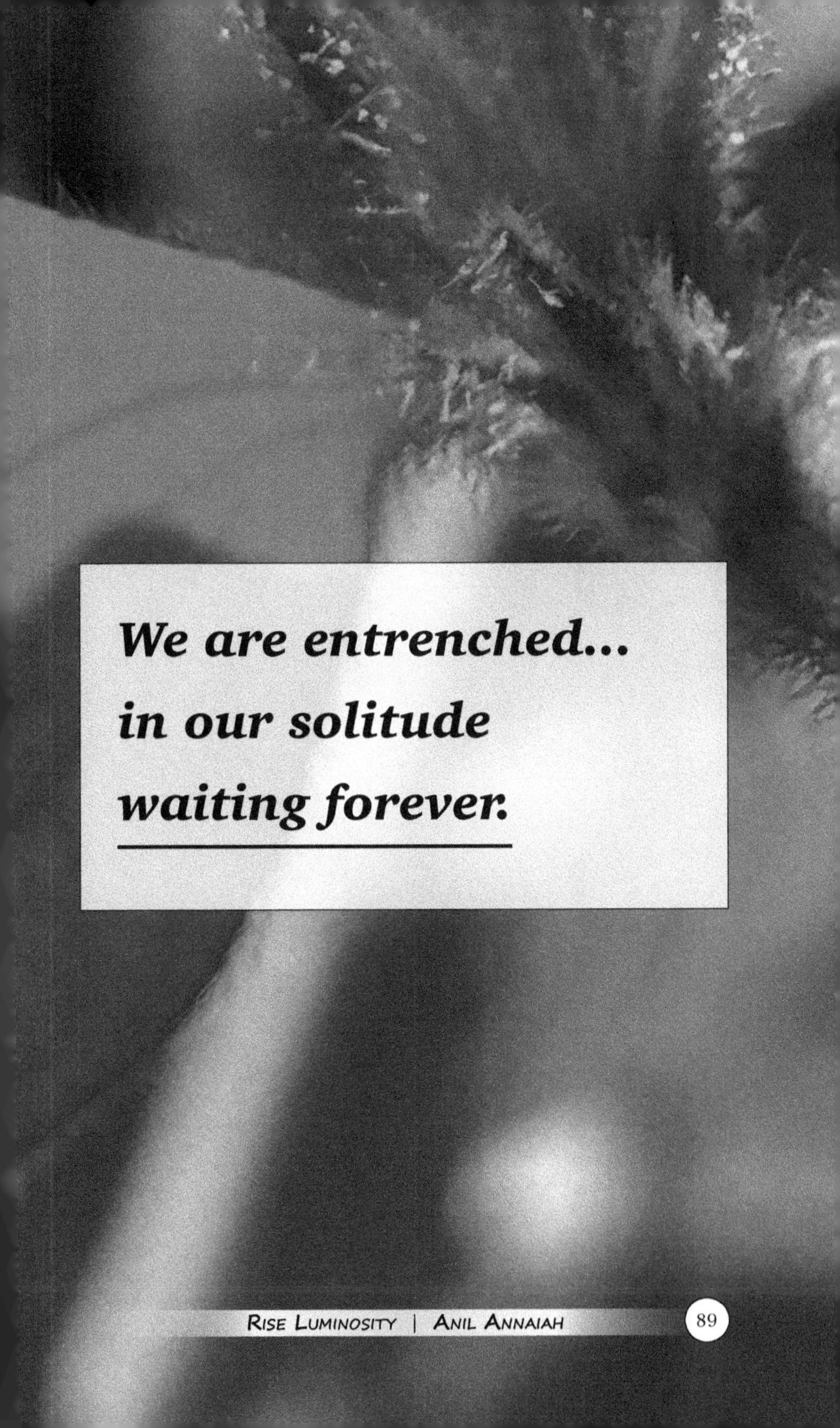

We are entrenched...
in our solitude
waiting forever.

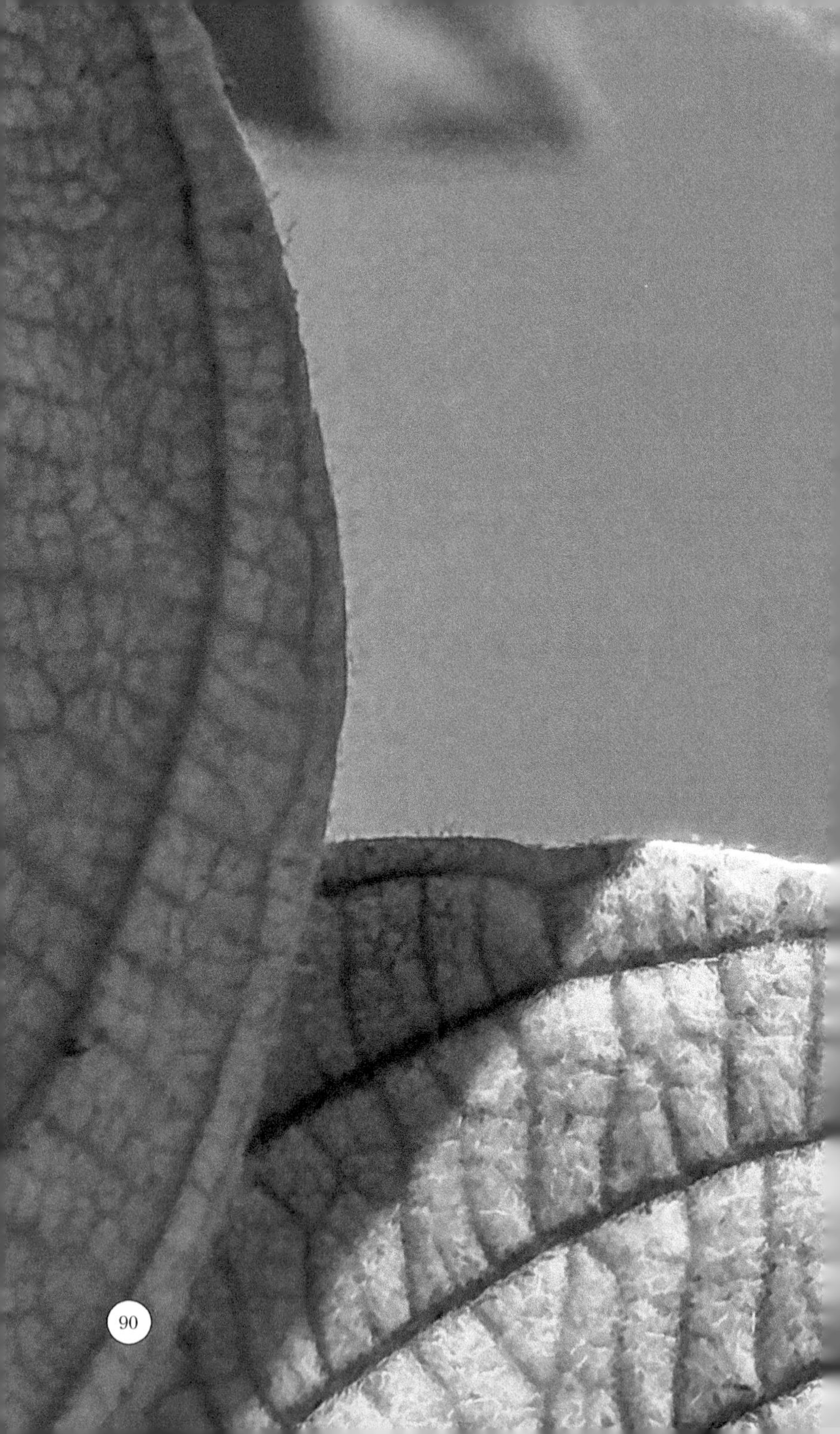

Desires come... with no limit on fallibility.

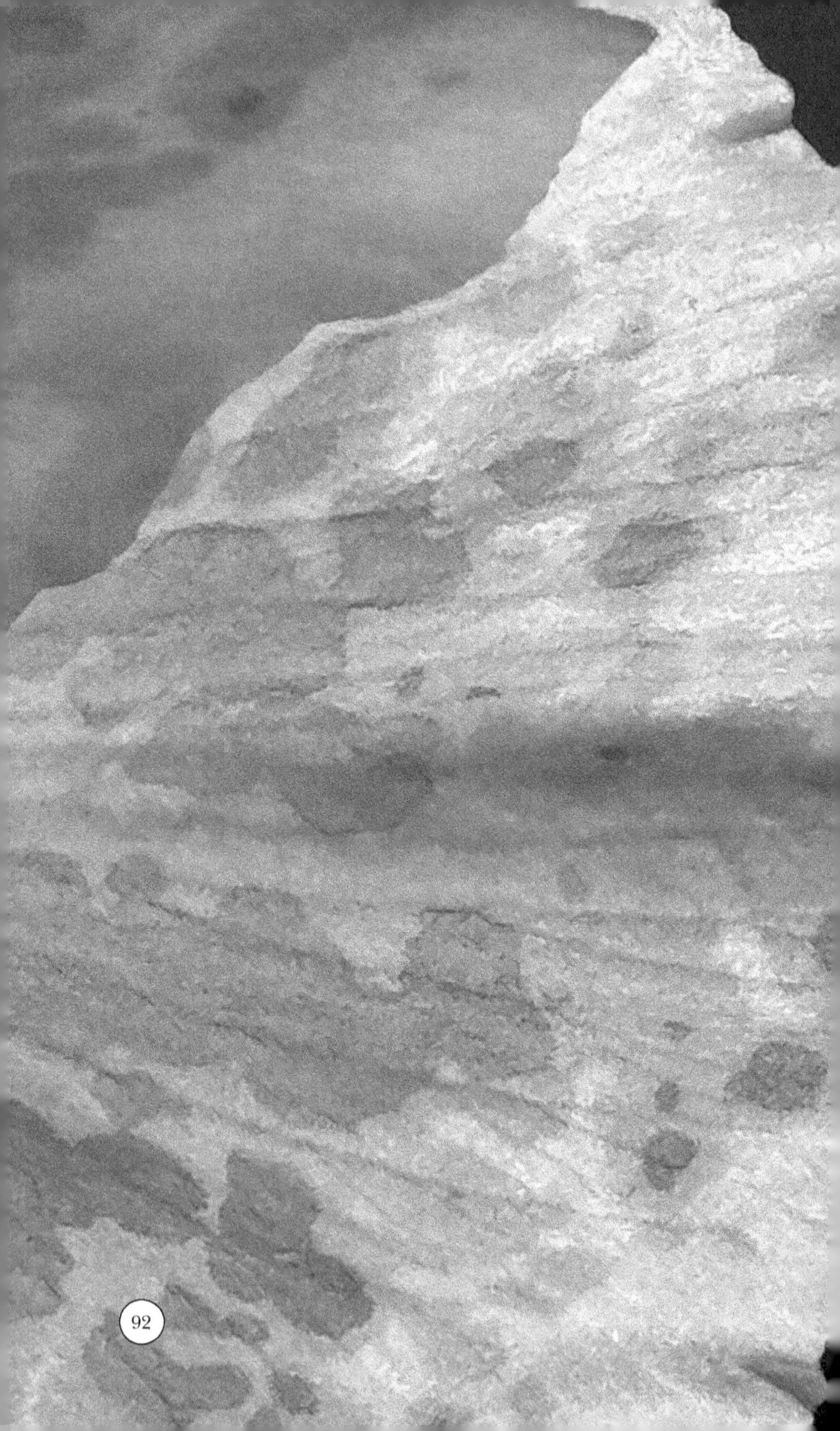

The storm clears the way... but leaves behind little.

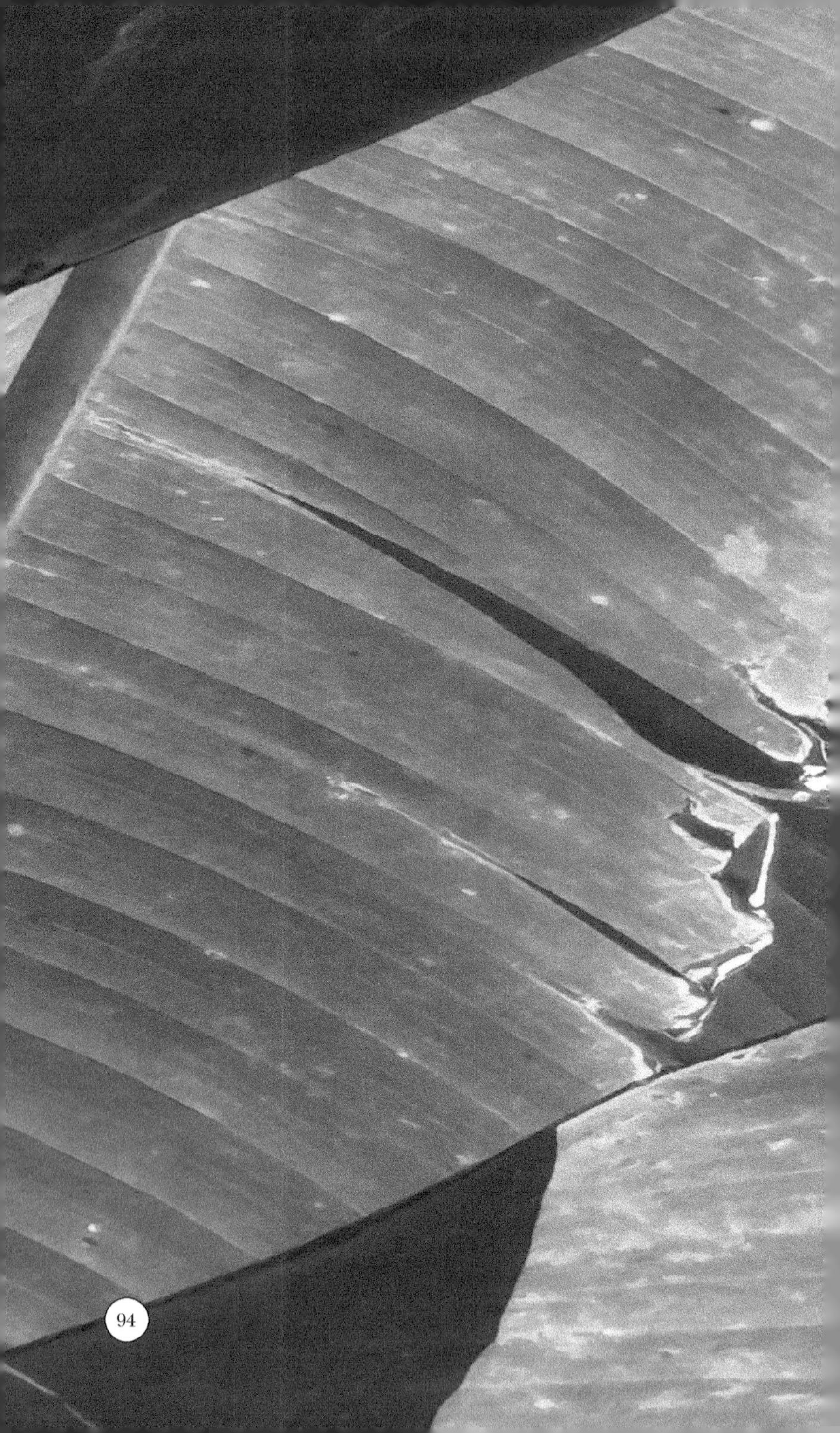

All battles are fought
at unequal paces...
but the effects remain
common.

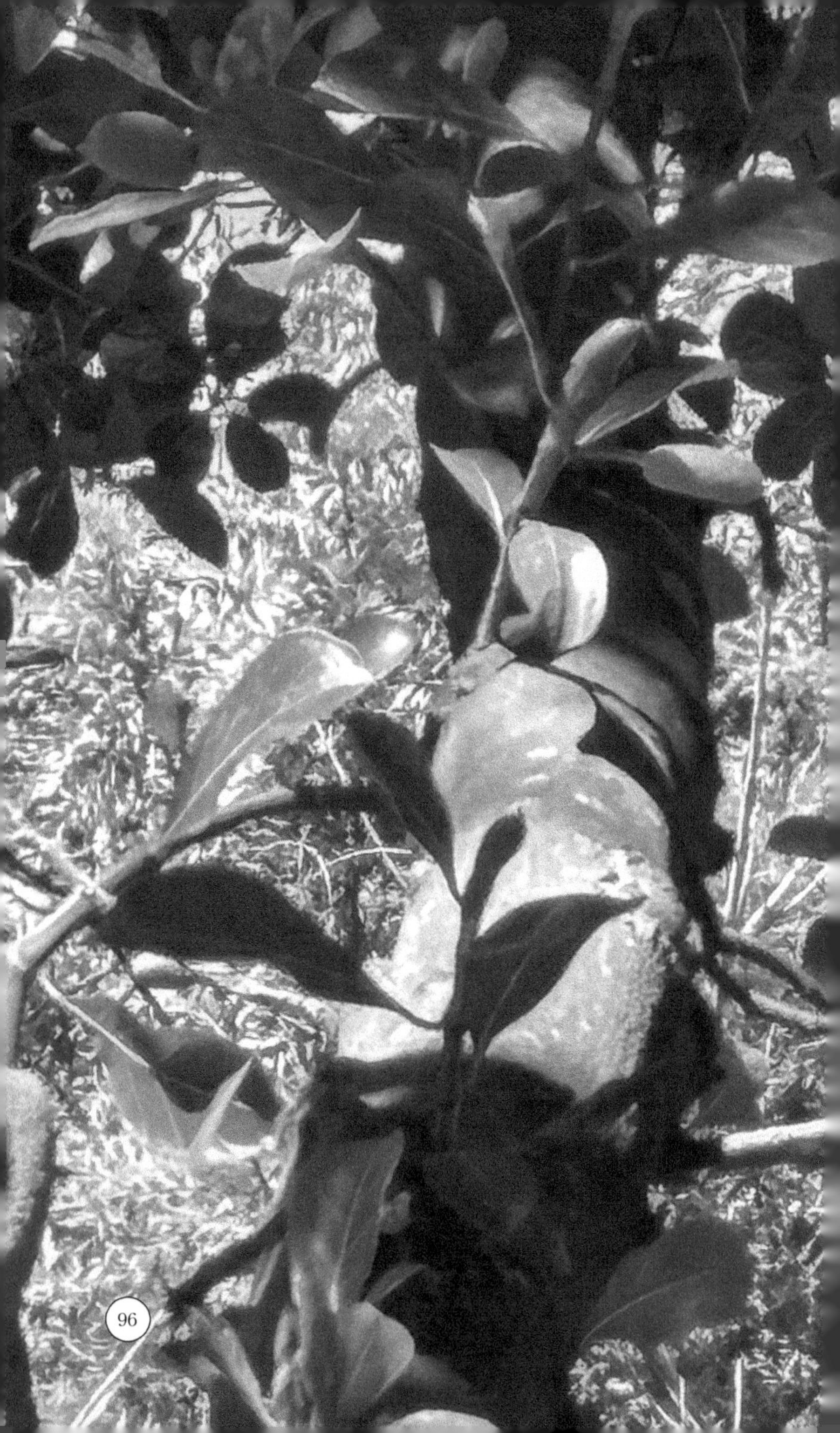

There will be no ropes to hold on to... if you have spent your time using the cover of darkness.

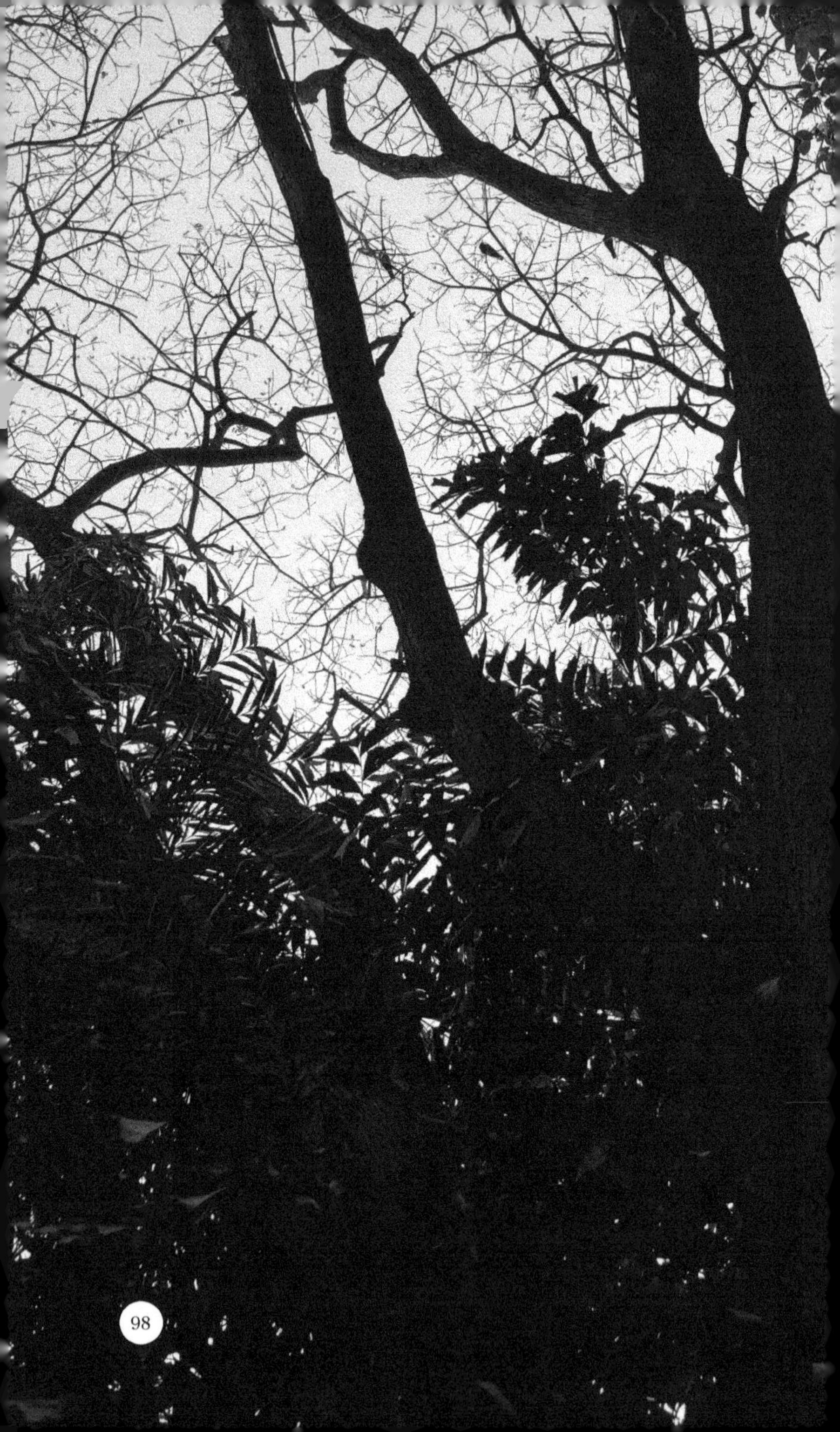

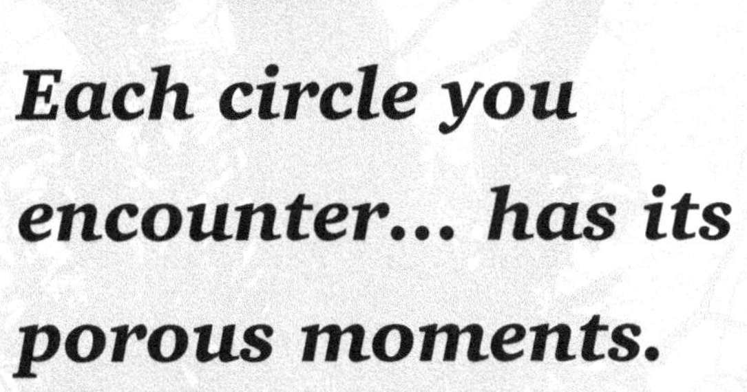

Each circle you encounter... has its porous moments.

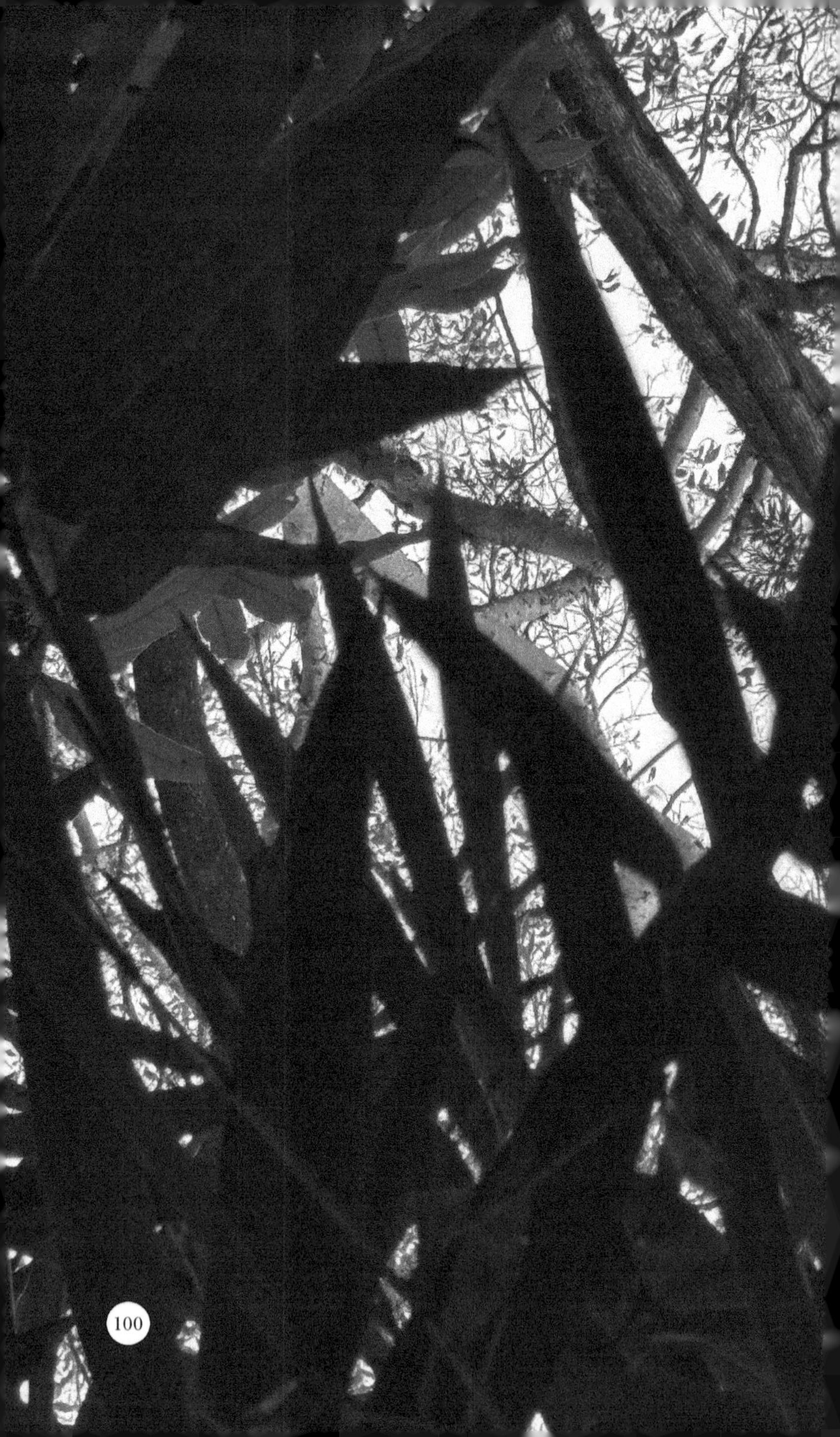

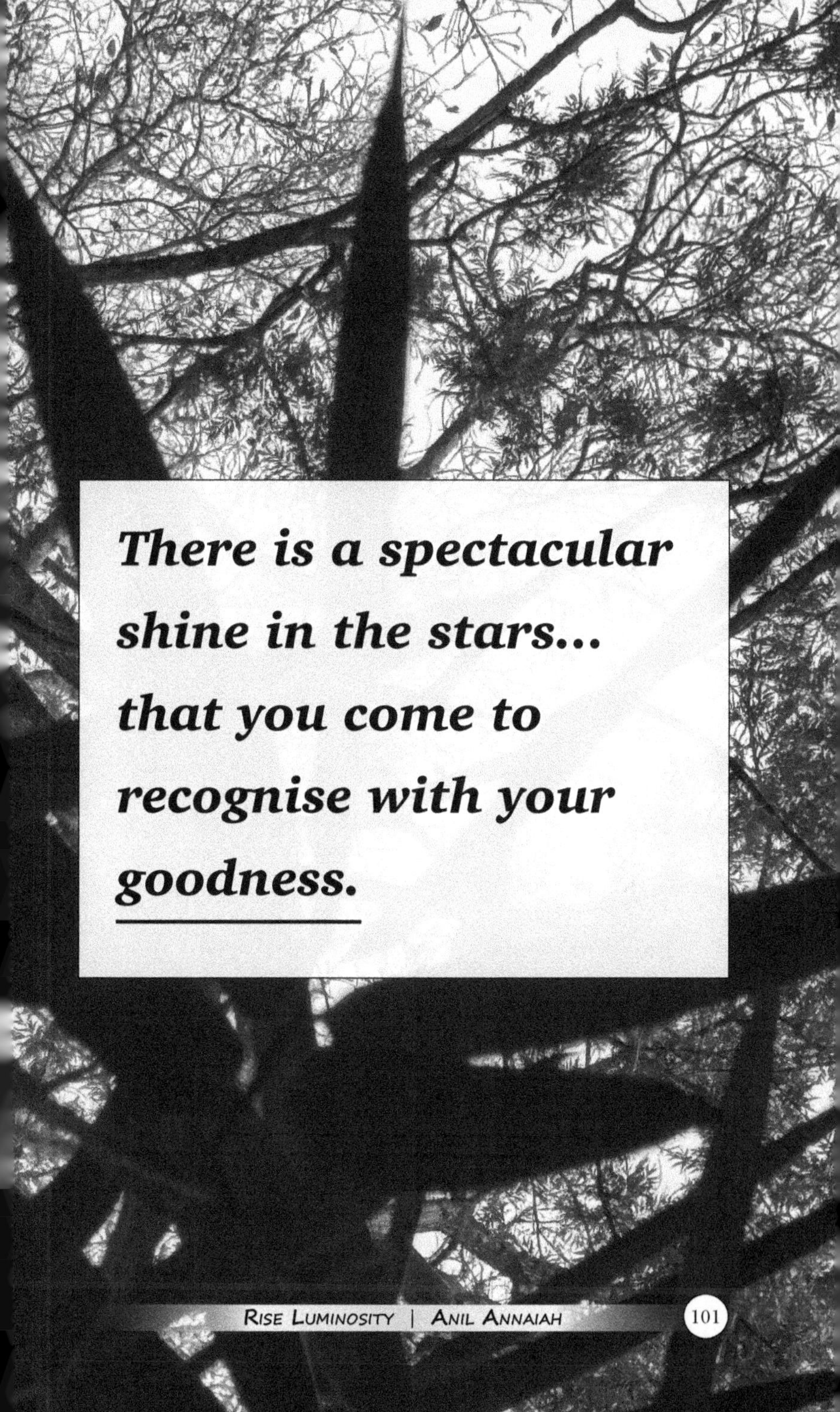

There is a spectacular shine in the stars... that you come to recognise with your goodness.

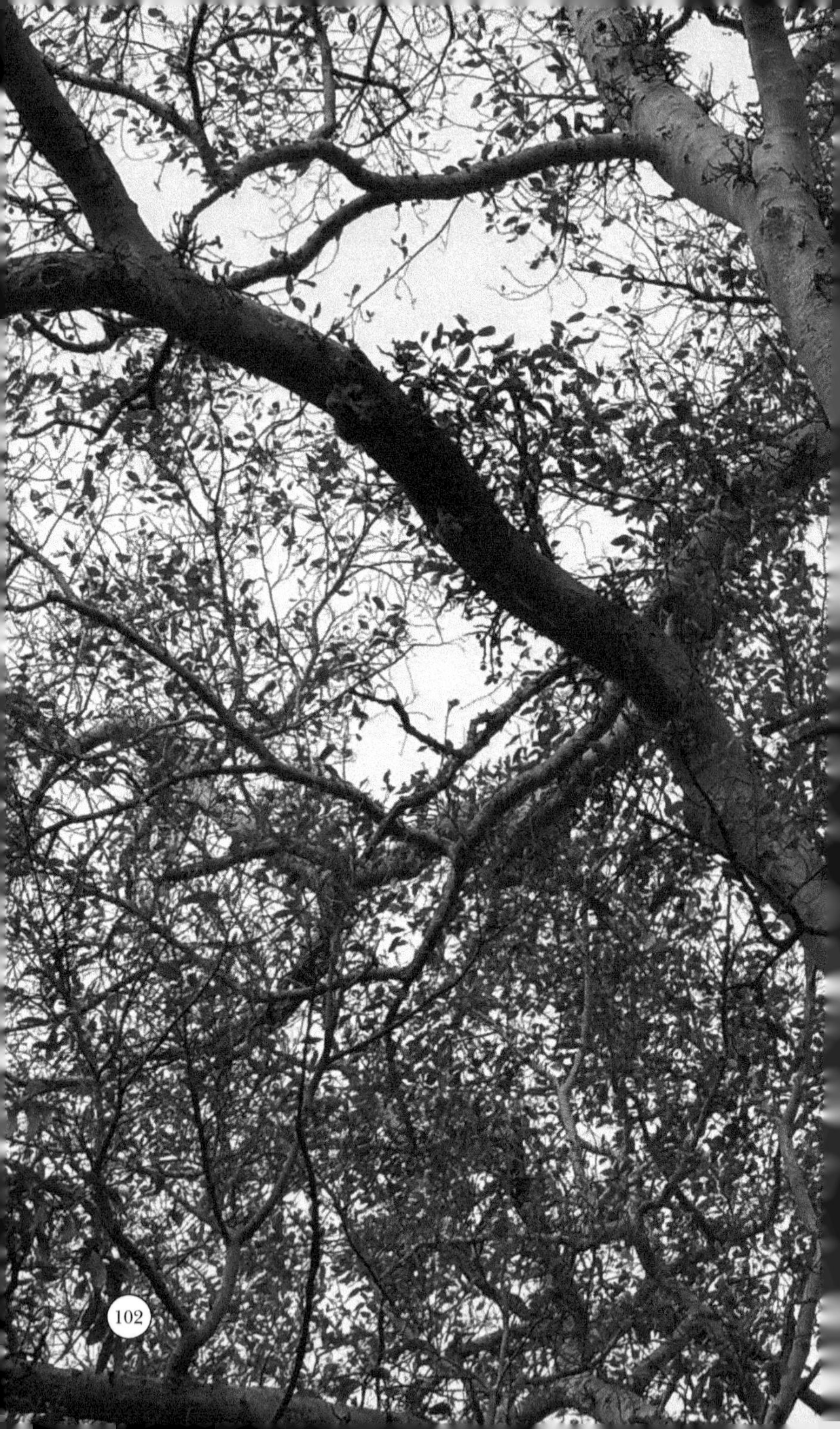

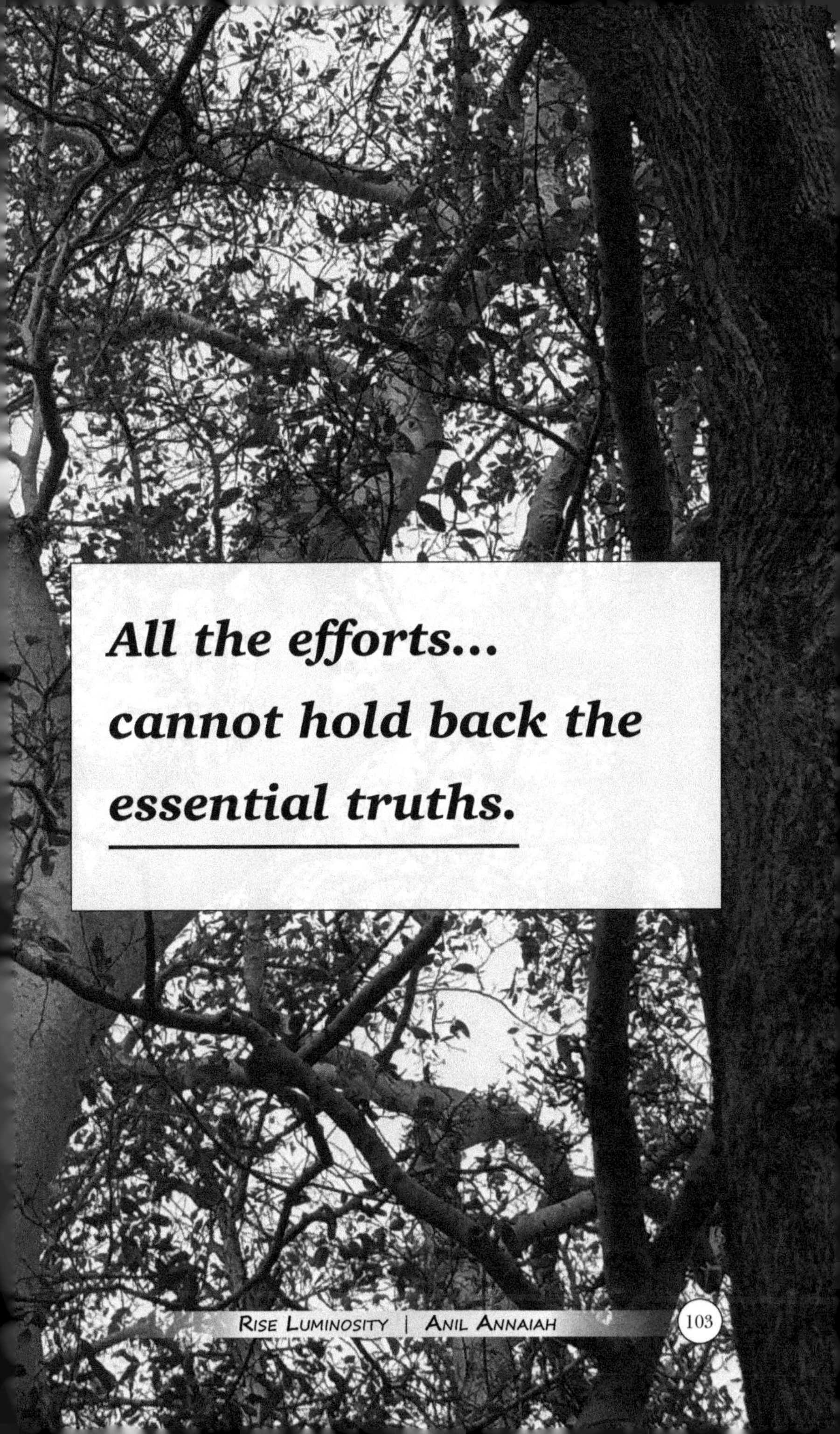

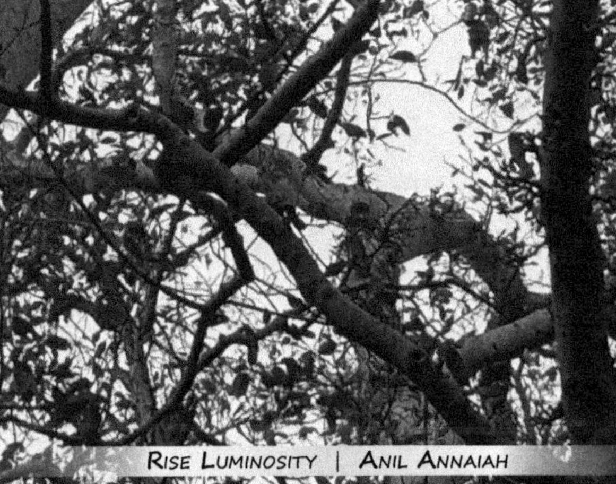

All the efforts...
cannot hold back the
essential truths.

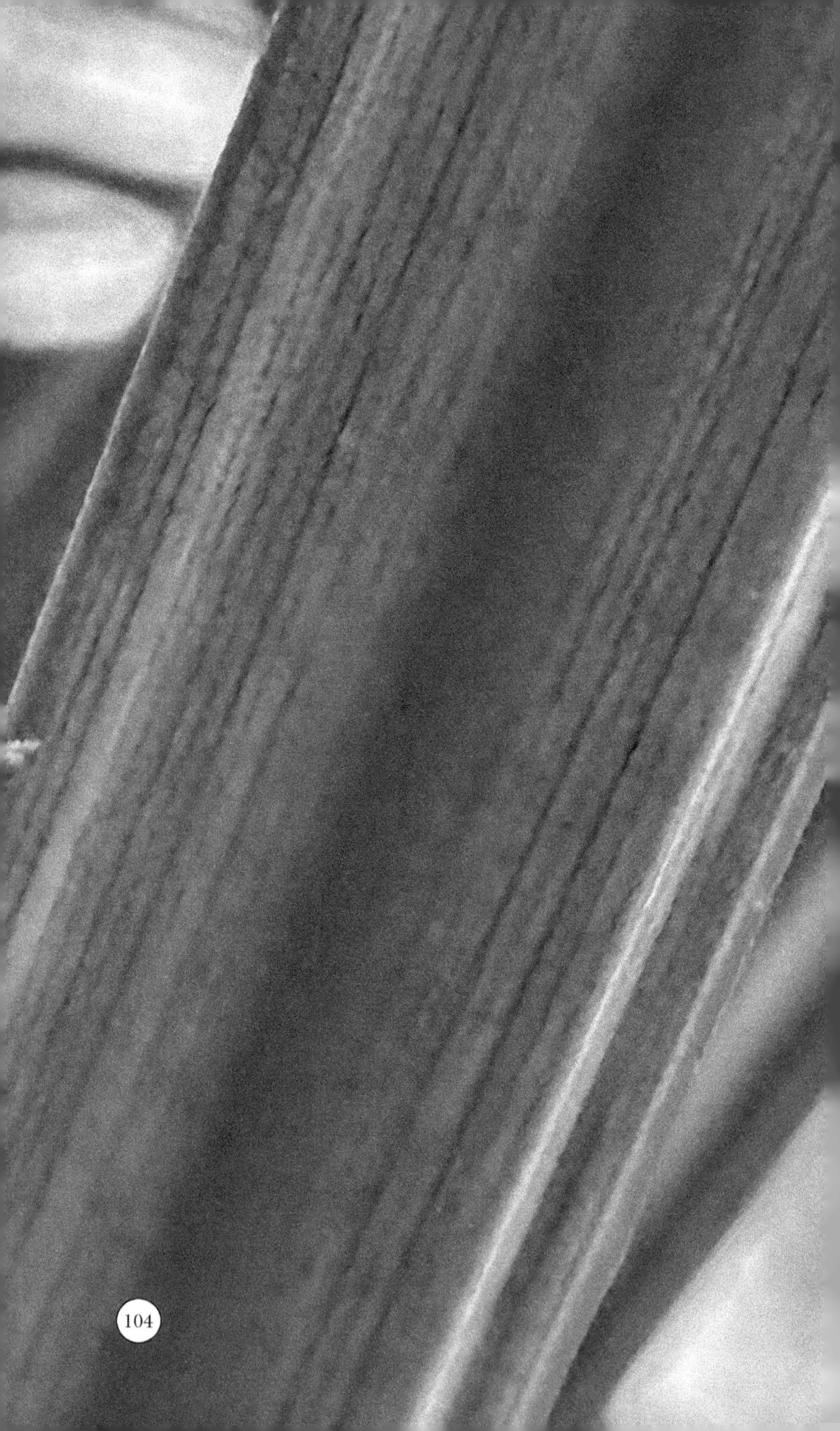

Be clear... let not doubt cease your mind.

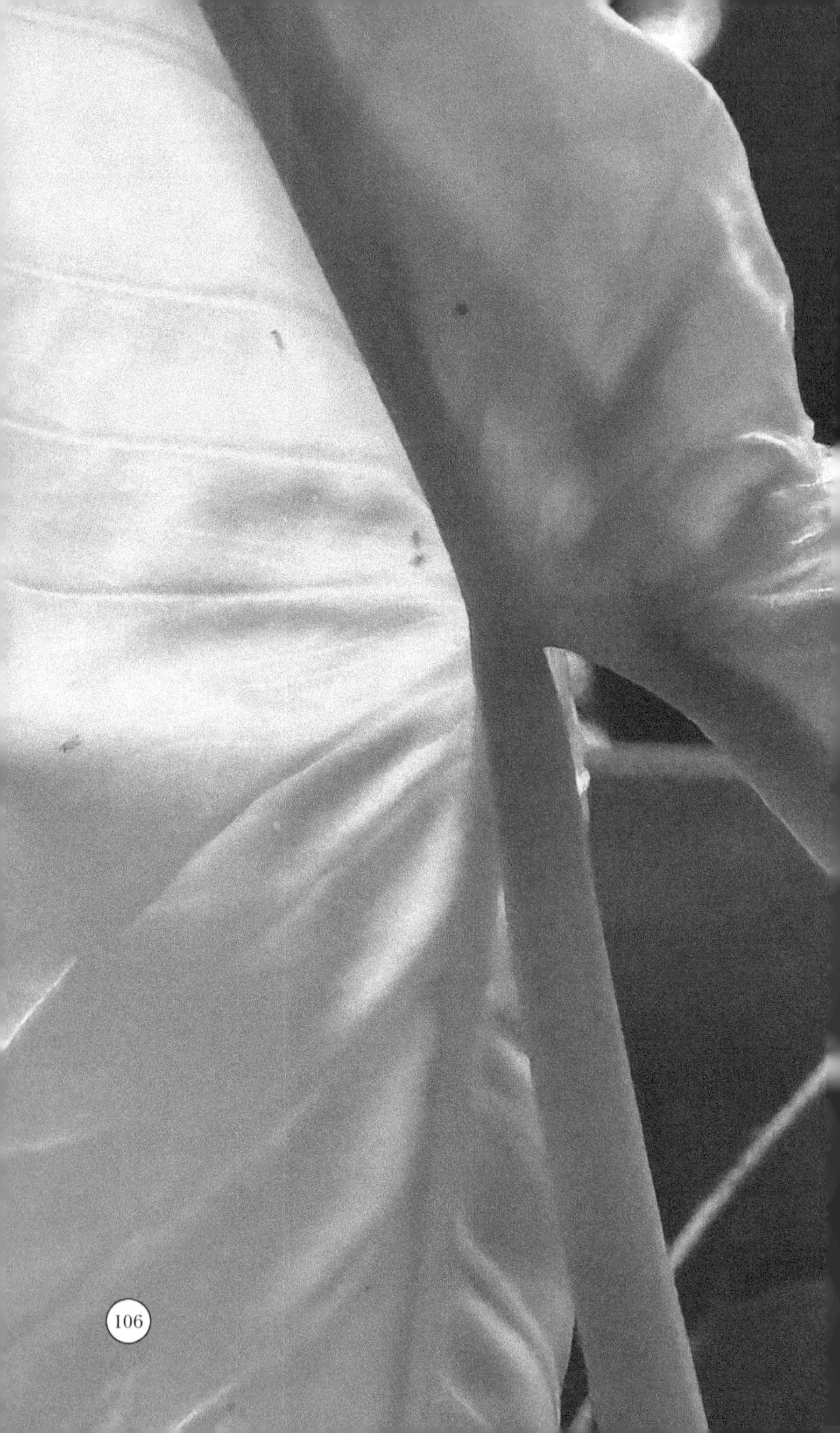

Maybe there is a dance... that some tunes look upon with disdain.

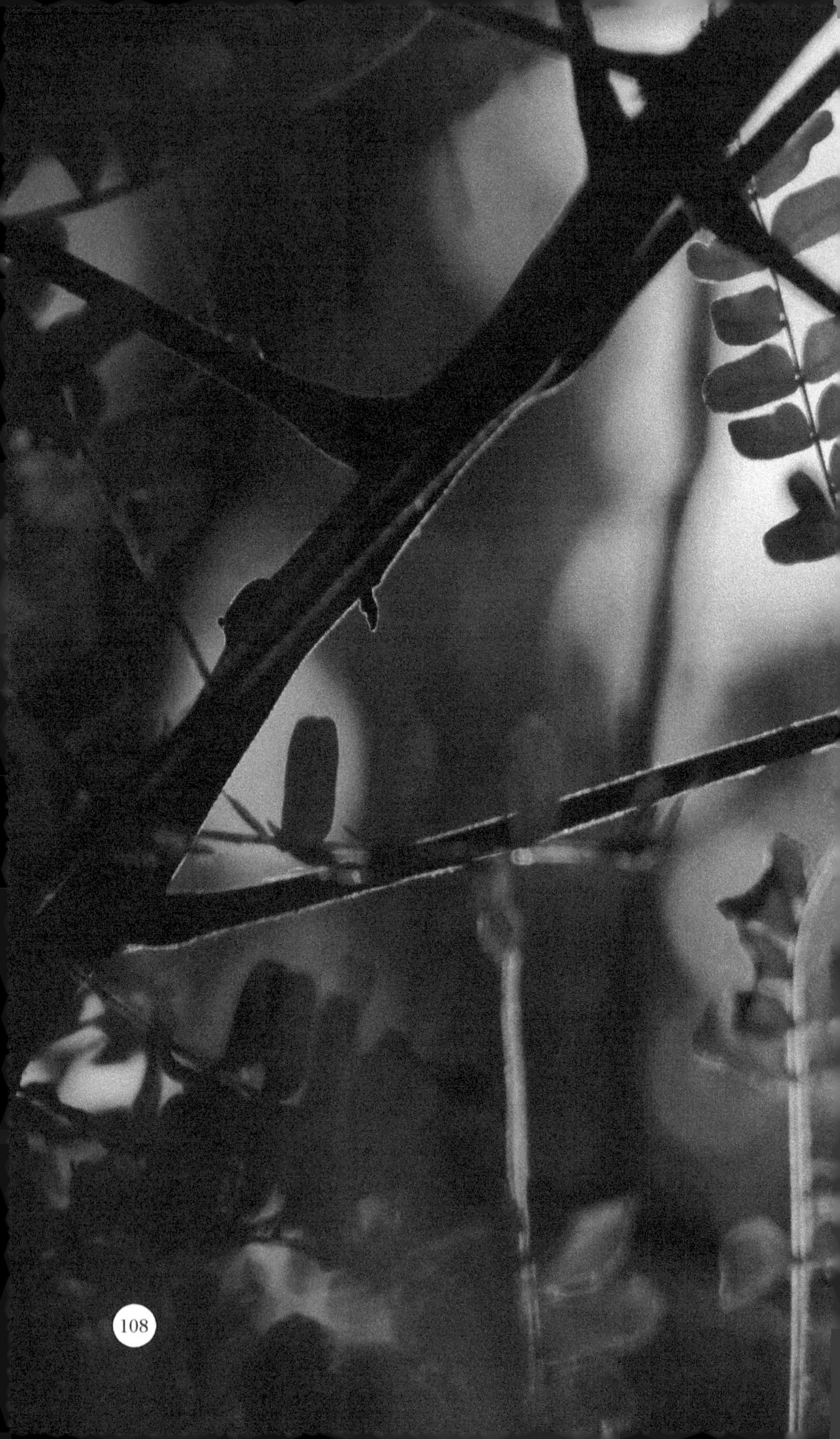

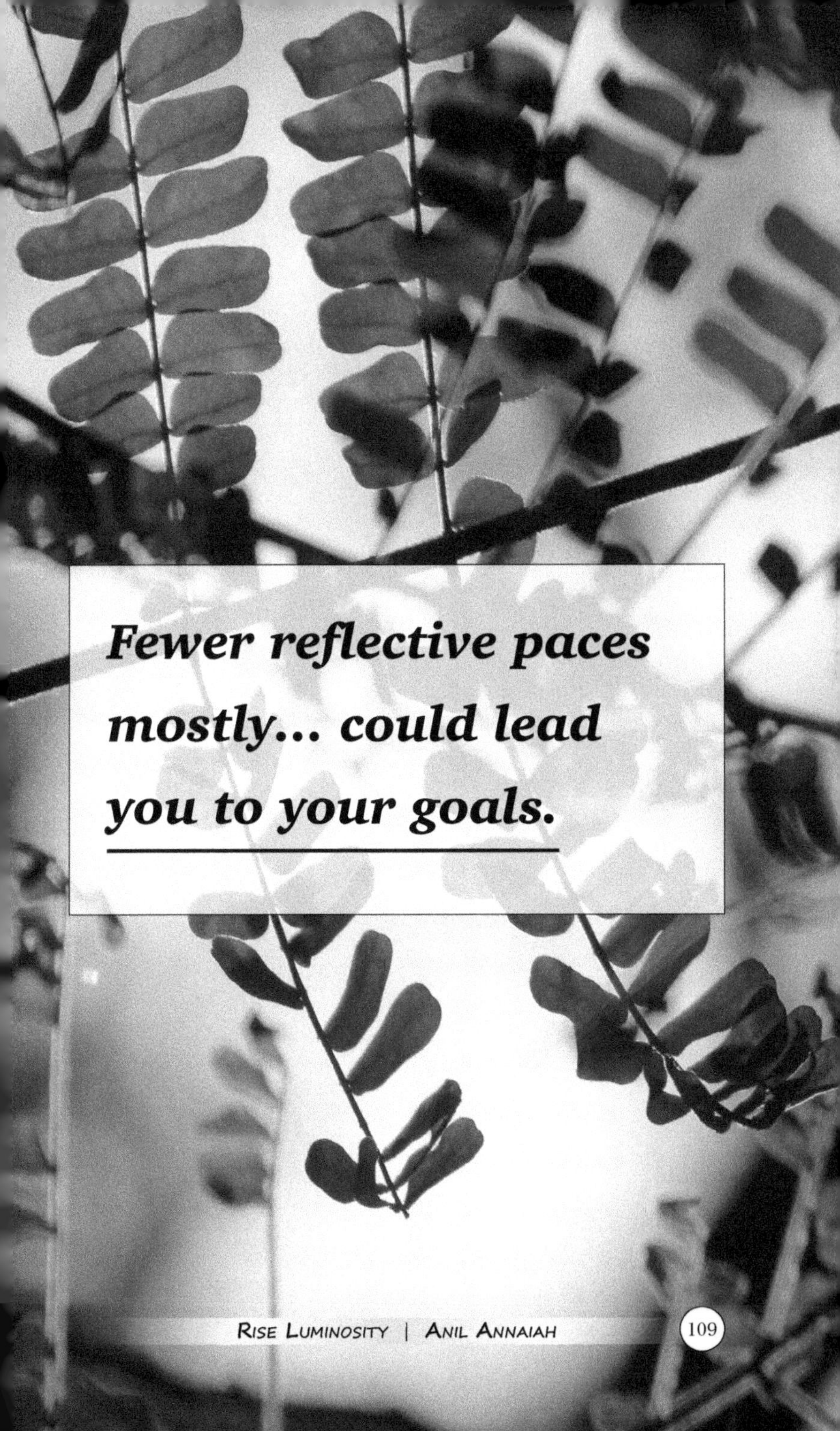

Fewer reflective paces mostly... could lead you to your goals.

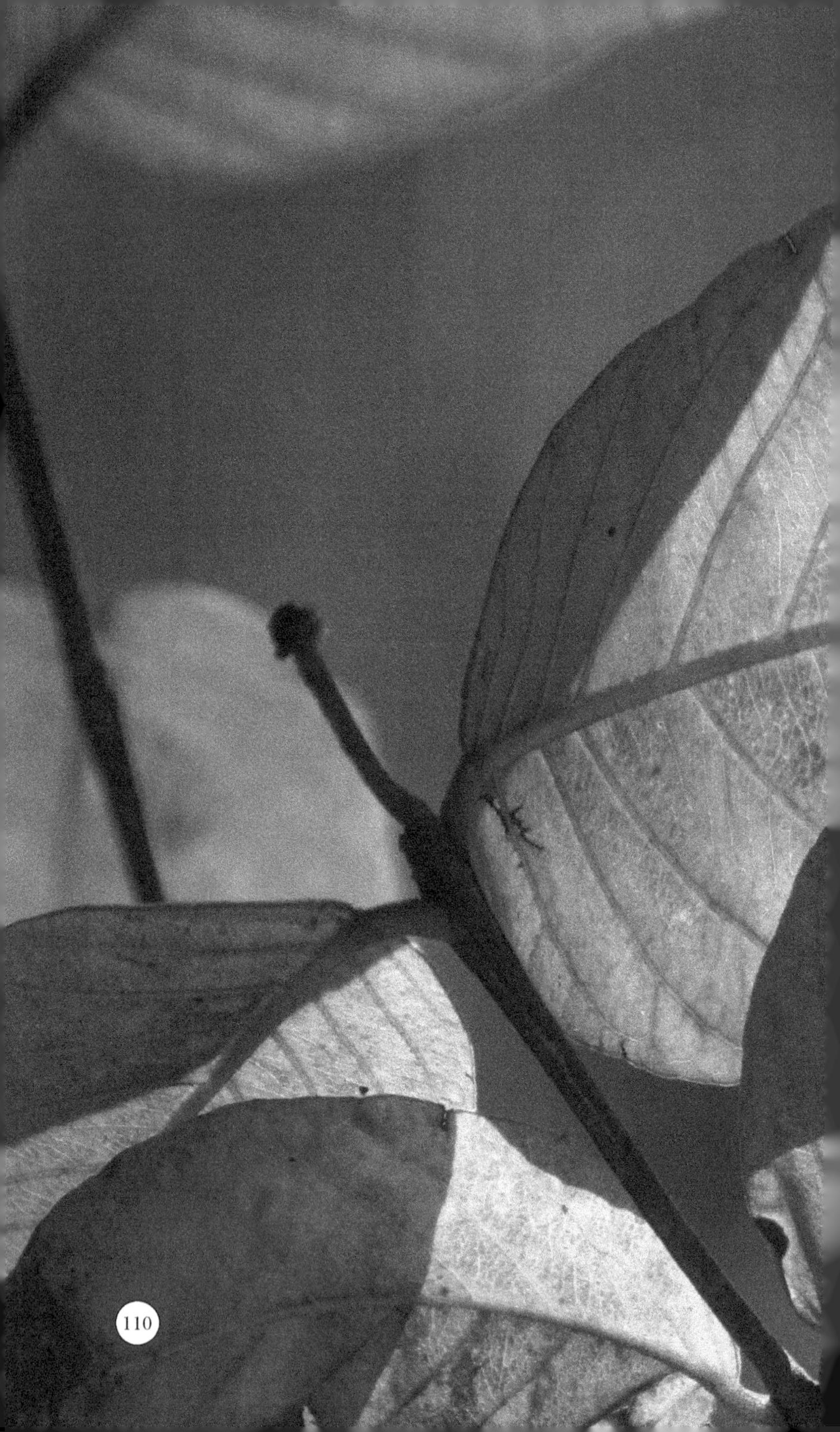

If you break through with your will... you must be truly sure of the direction.

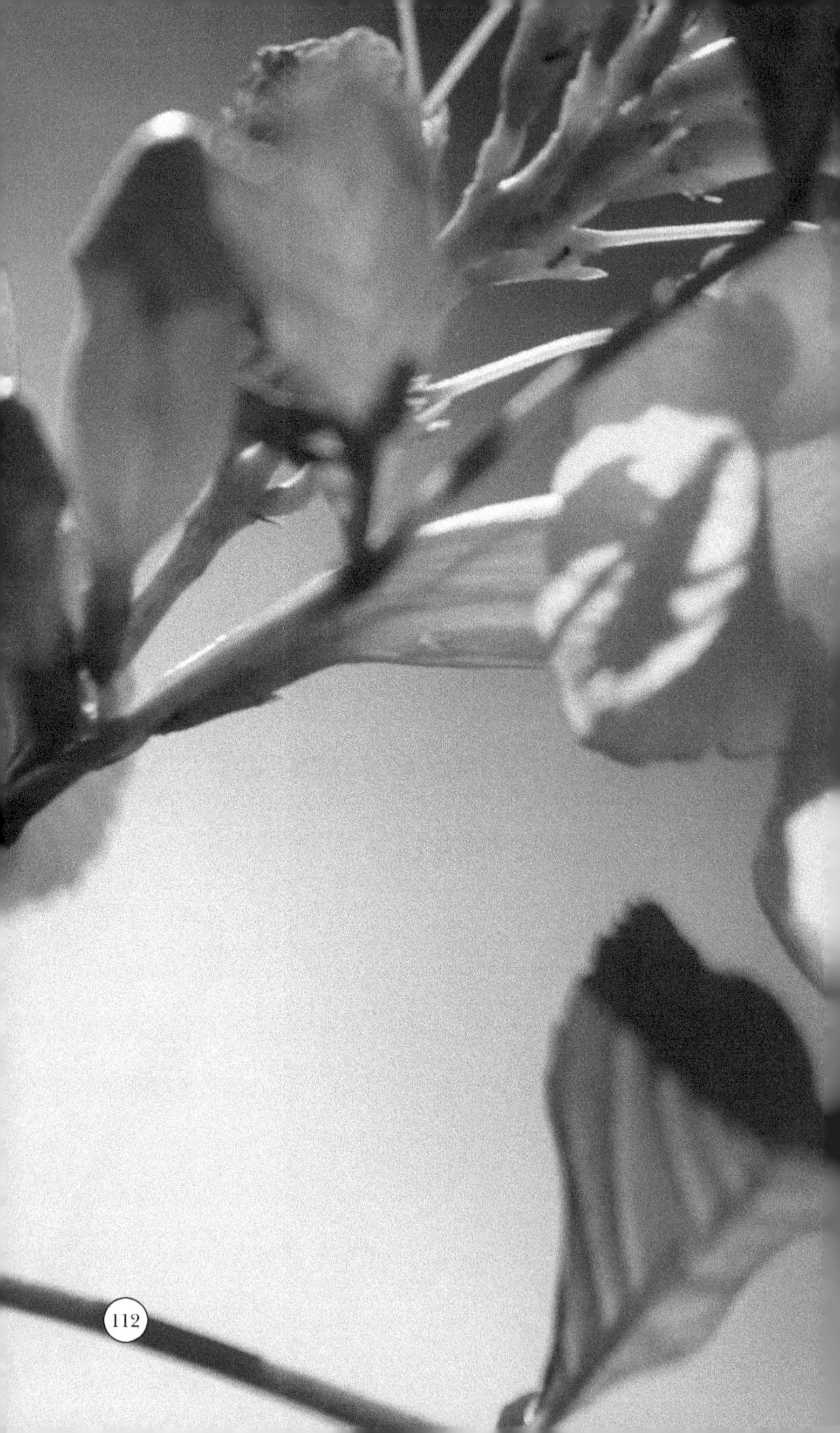

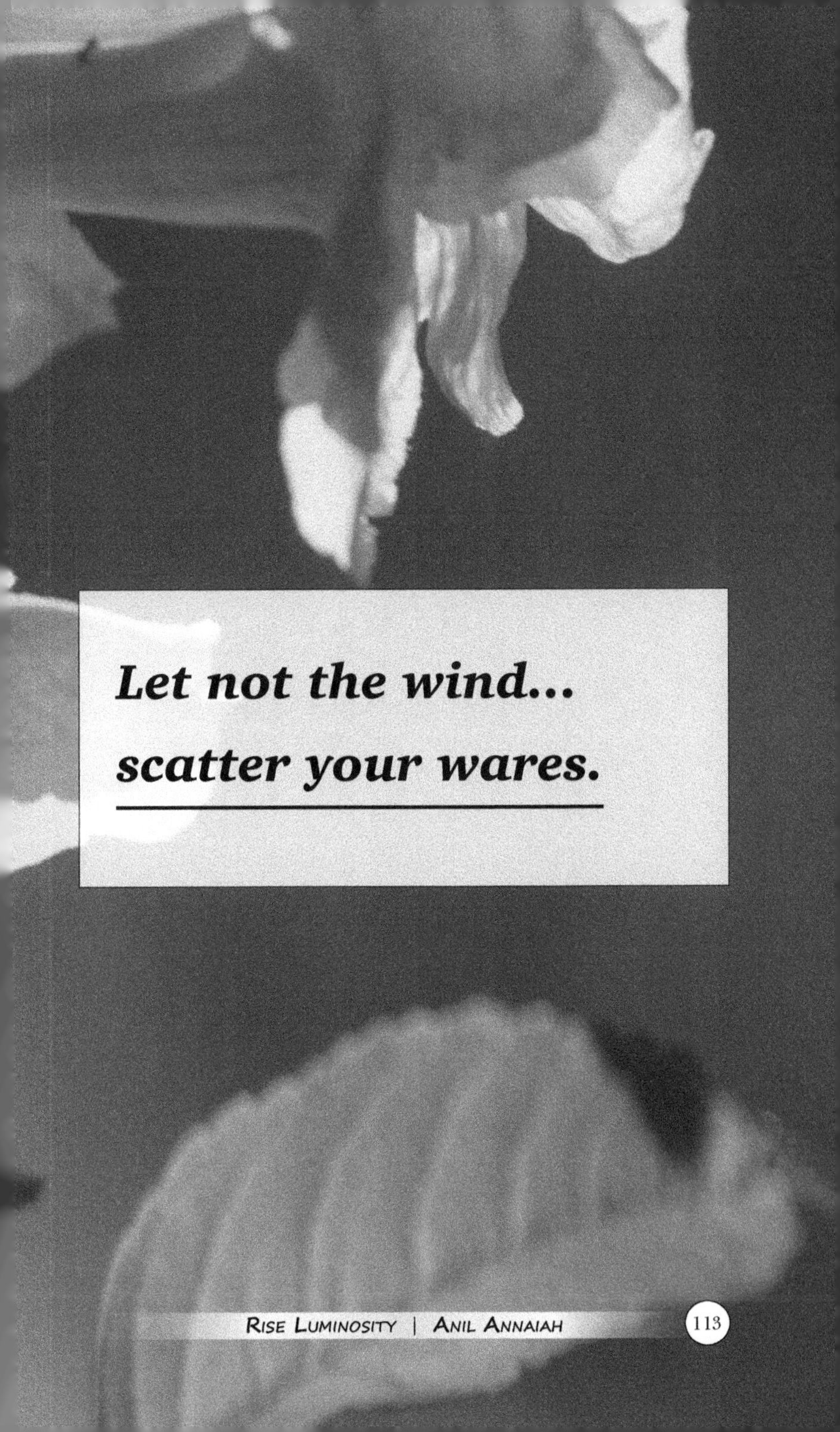

Let not the wind...
scatter your wares.

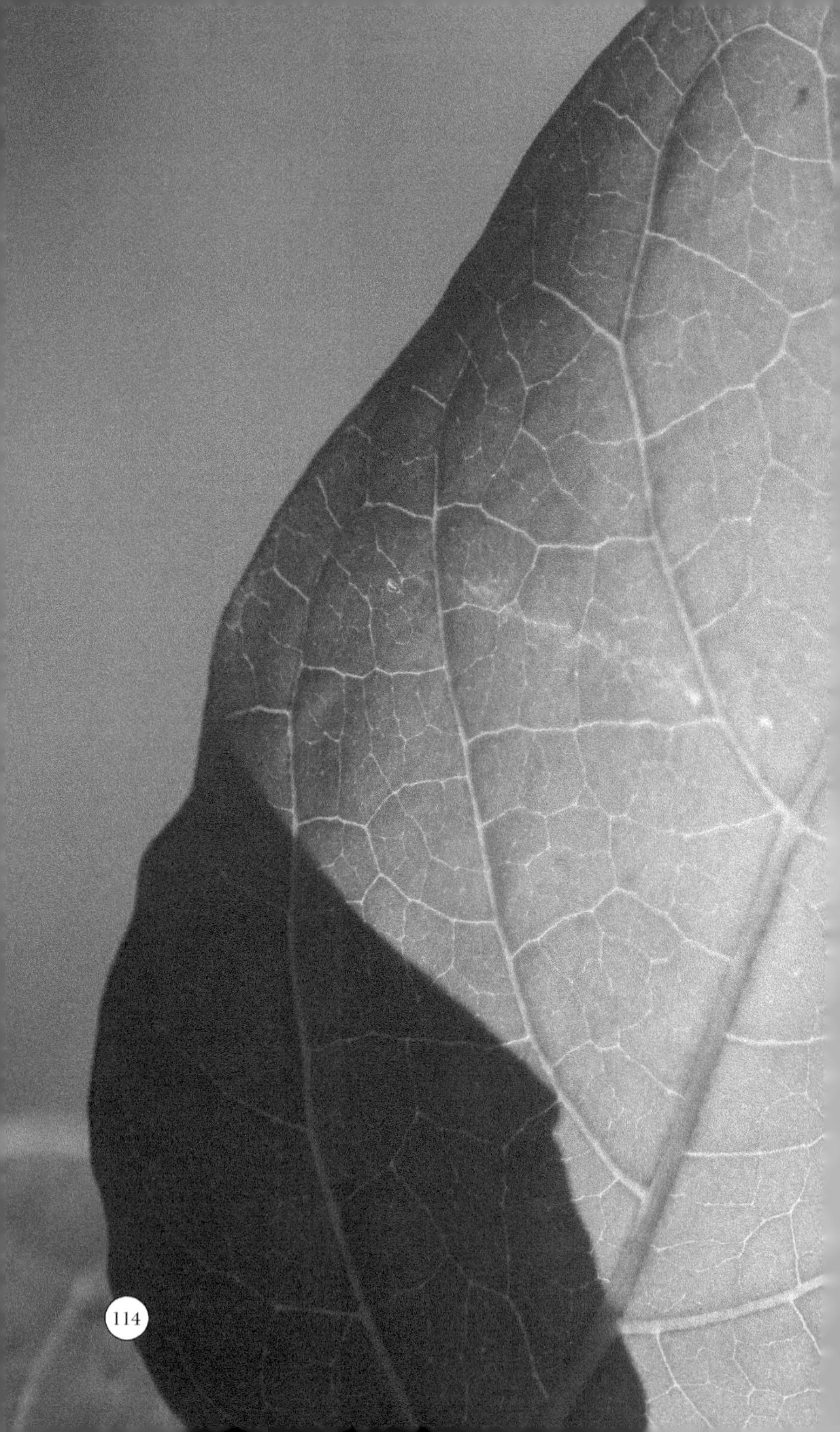

There are times... when you should decide... if your mind must move with the mountains or stay still.

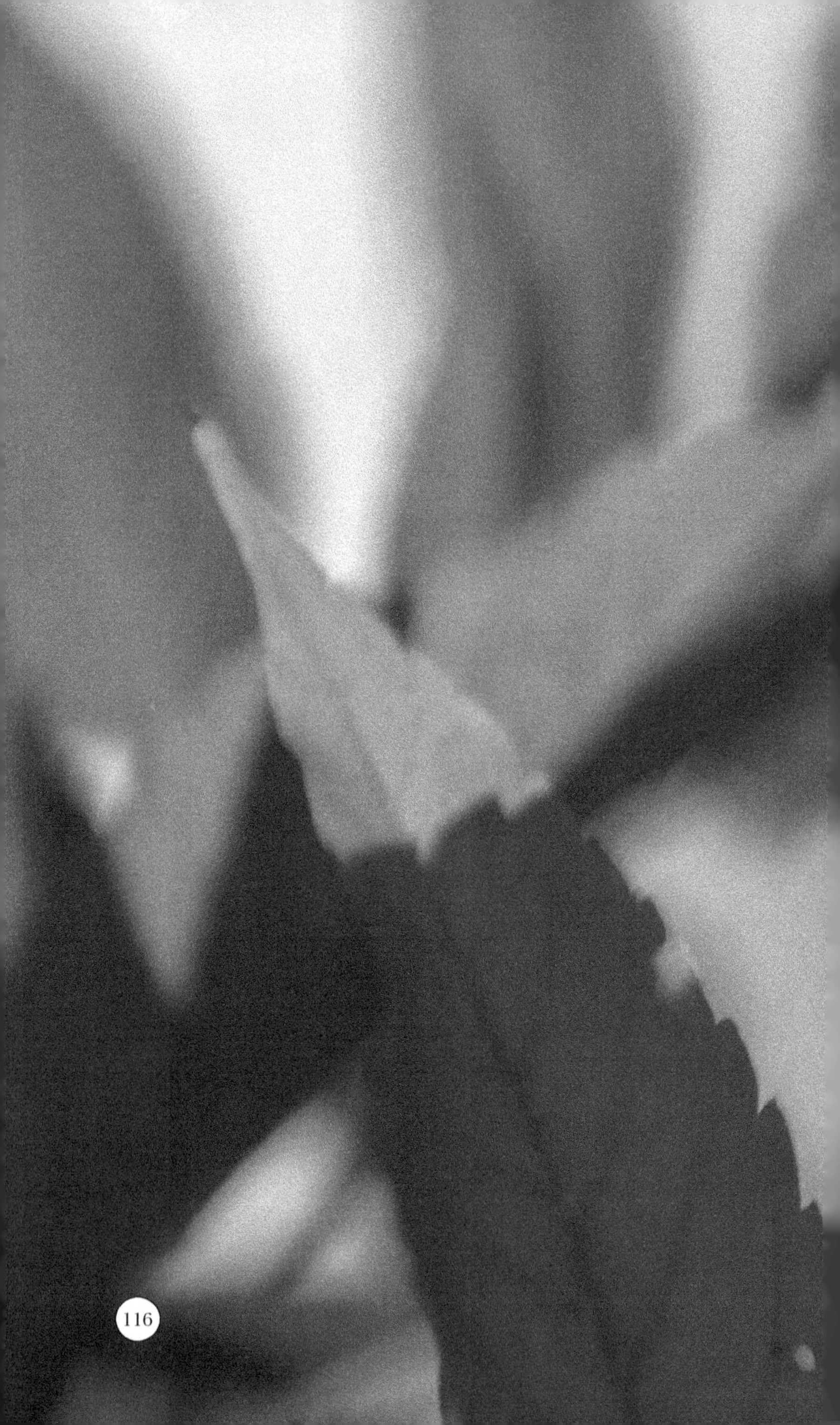

Learn to keep your hands free... from the shackles of time.

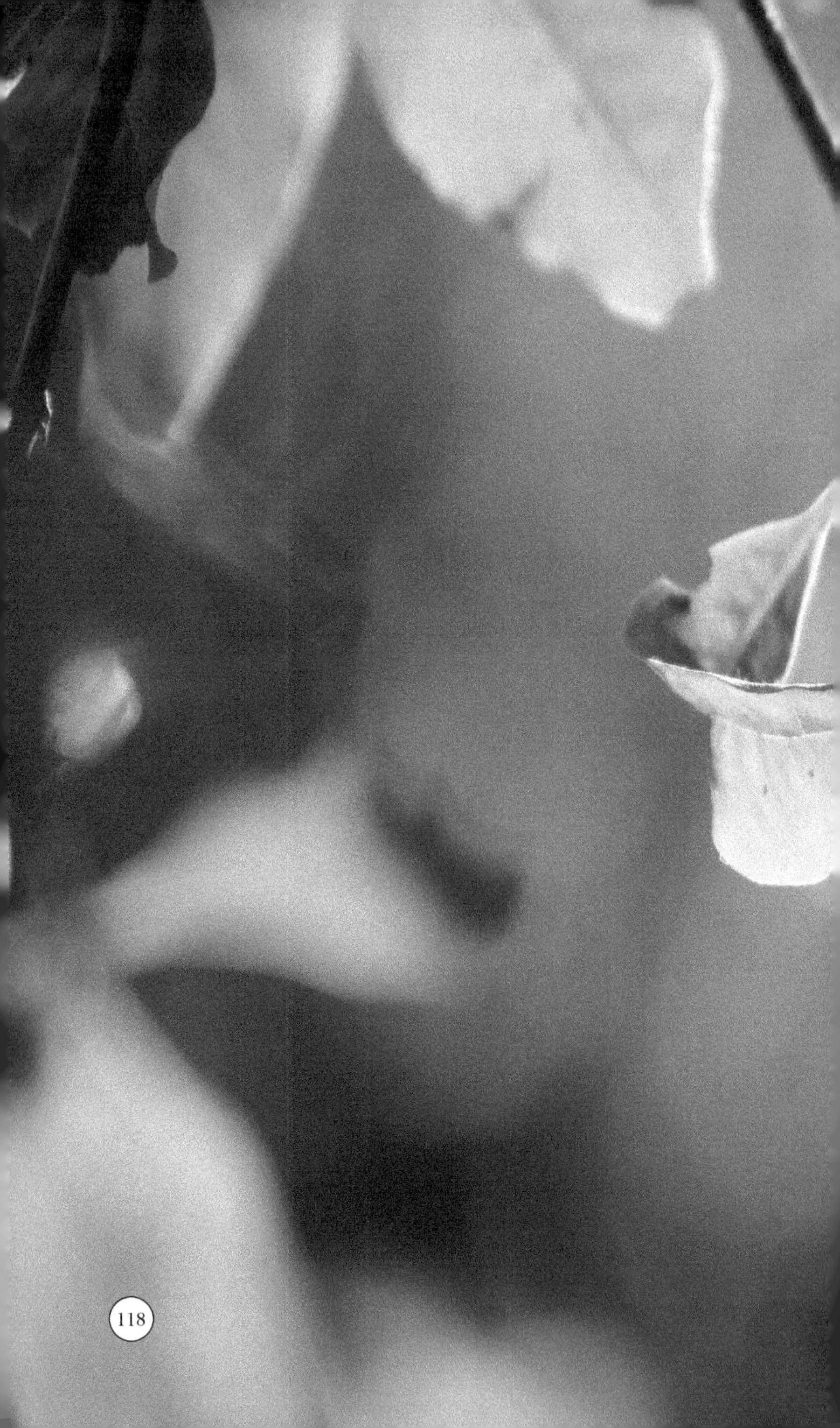

Your focus... needs your absolute presence.

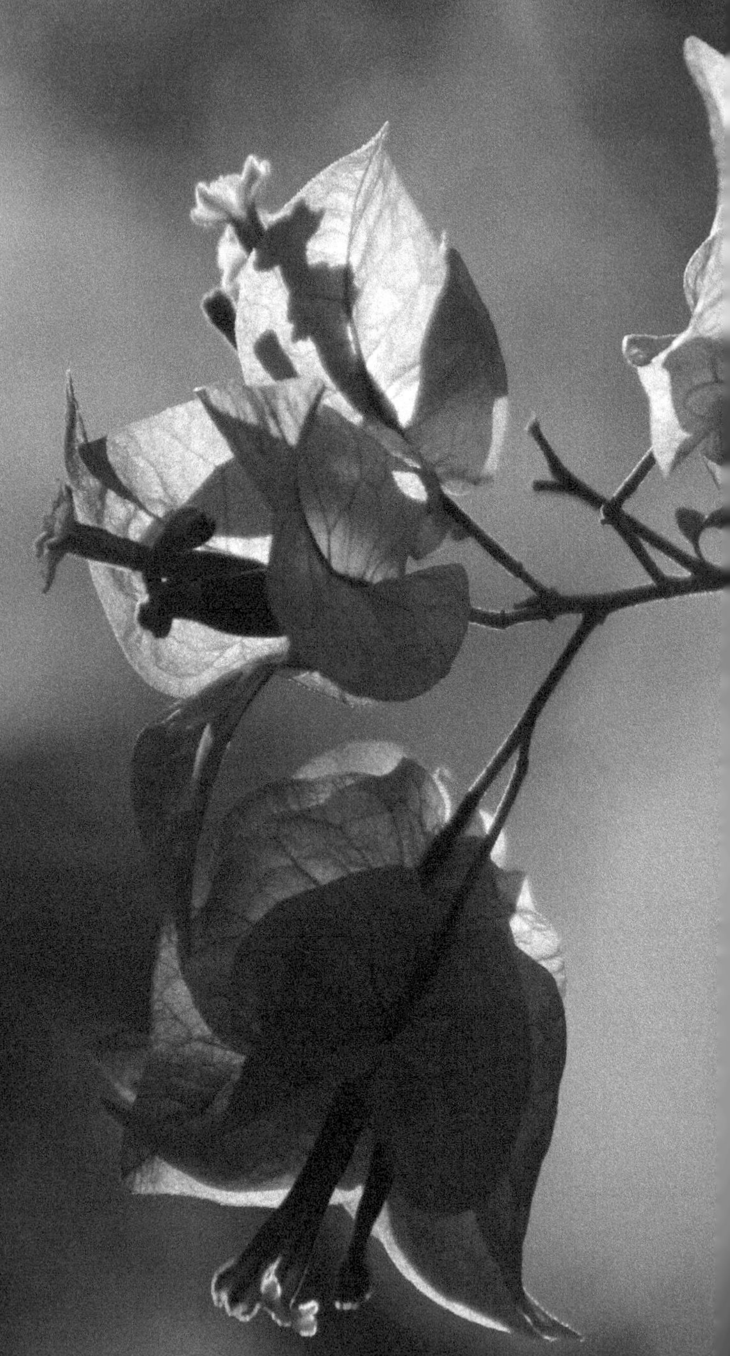

Do you mean well at every obstacle... to move forward at every juncture.

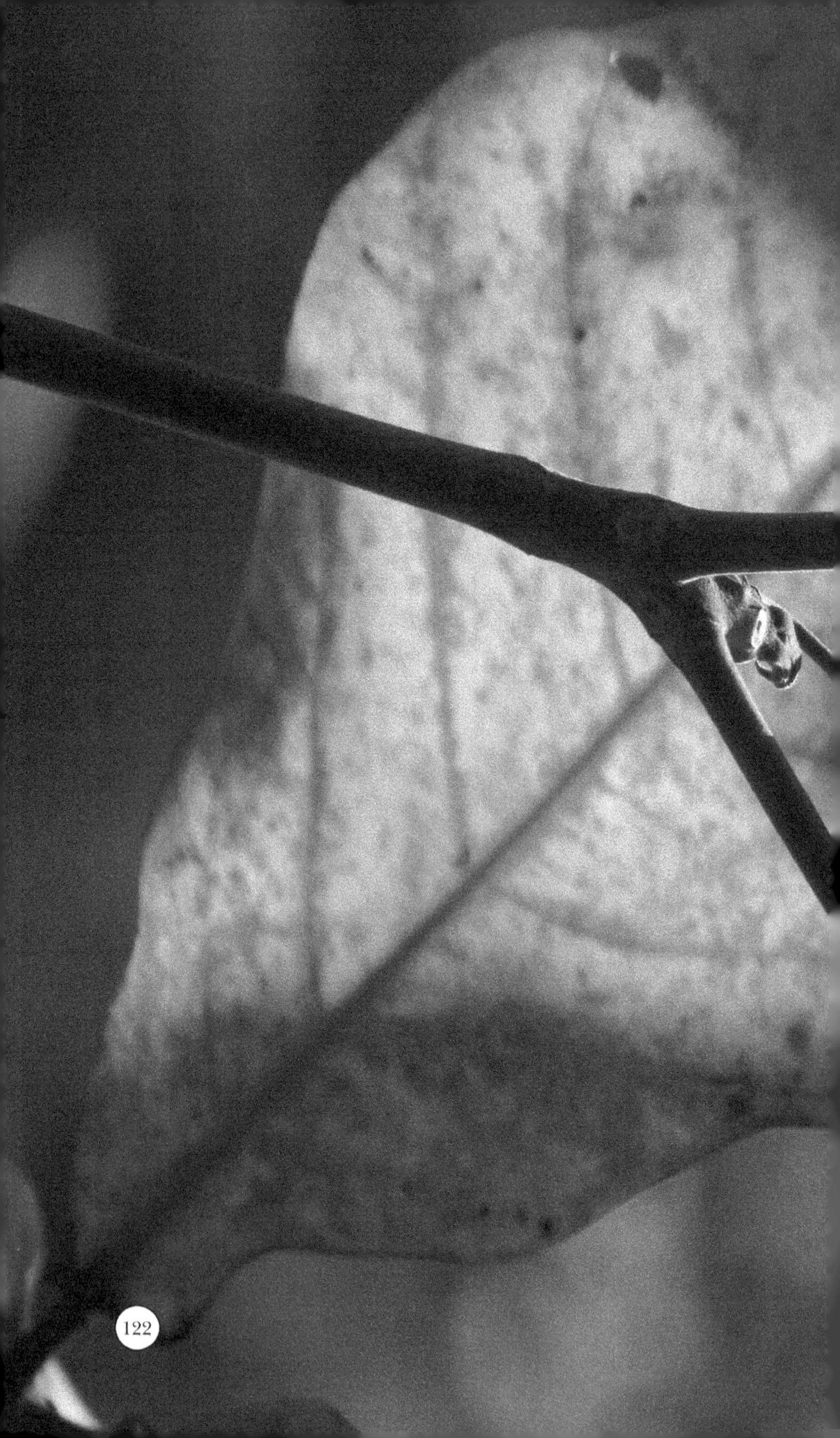

Let your dreams not remain in the space... that challenges reality.

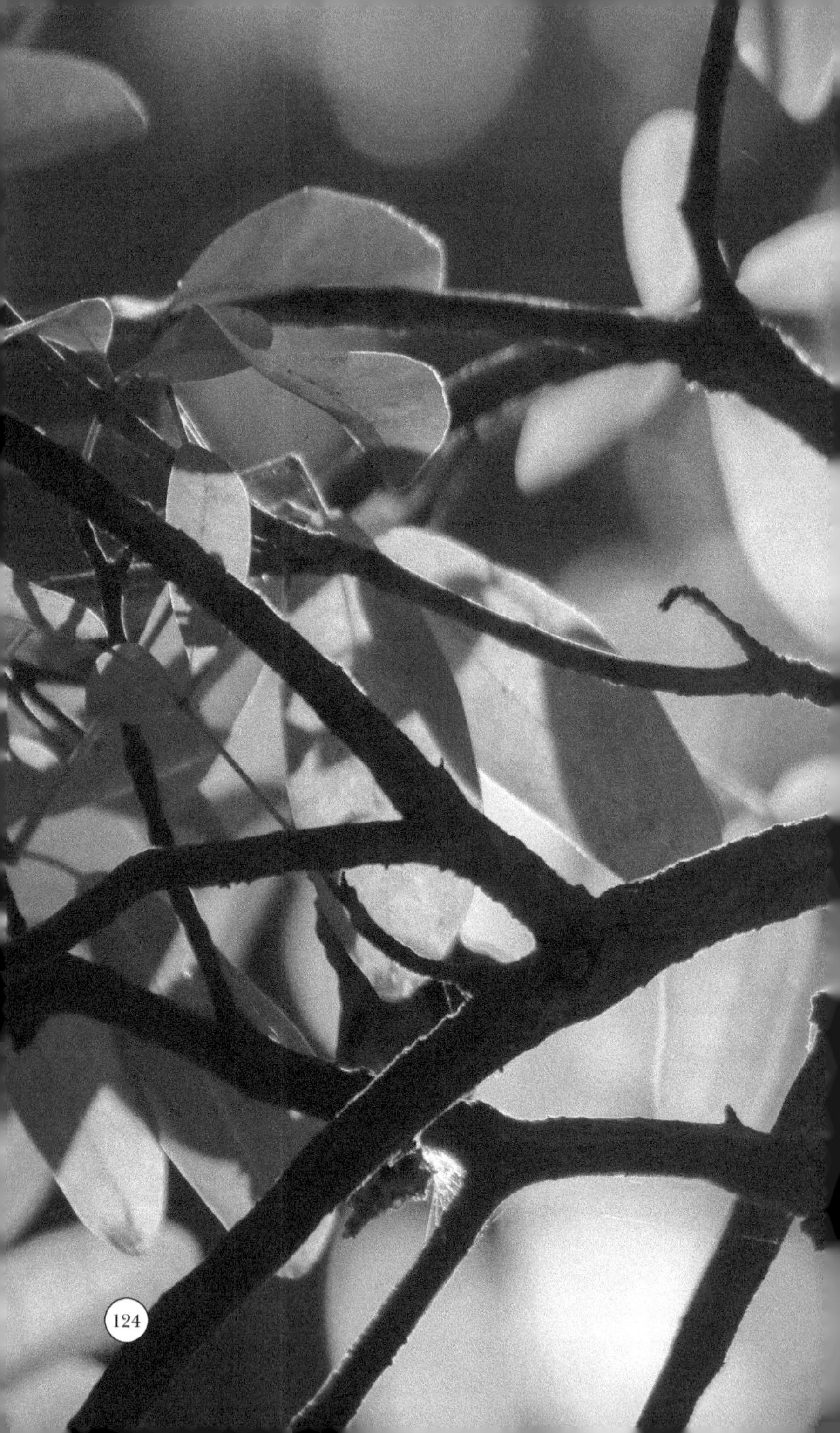

Is the sky blue enough... for you to see yourself through it.

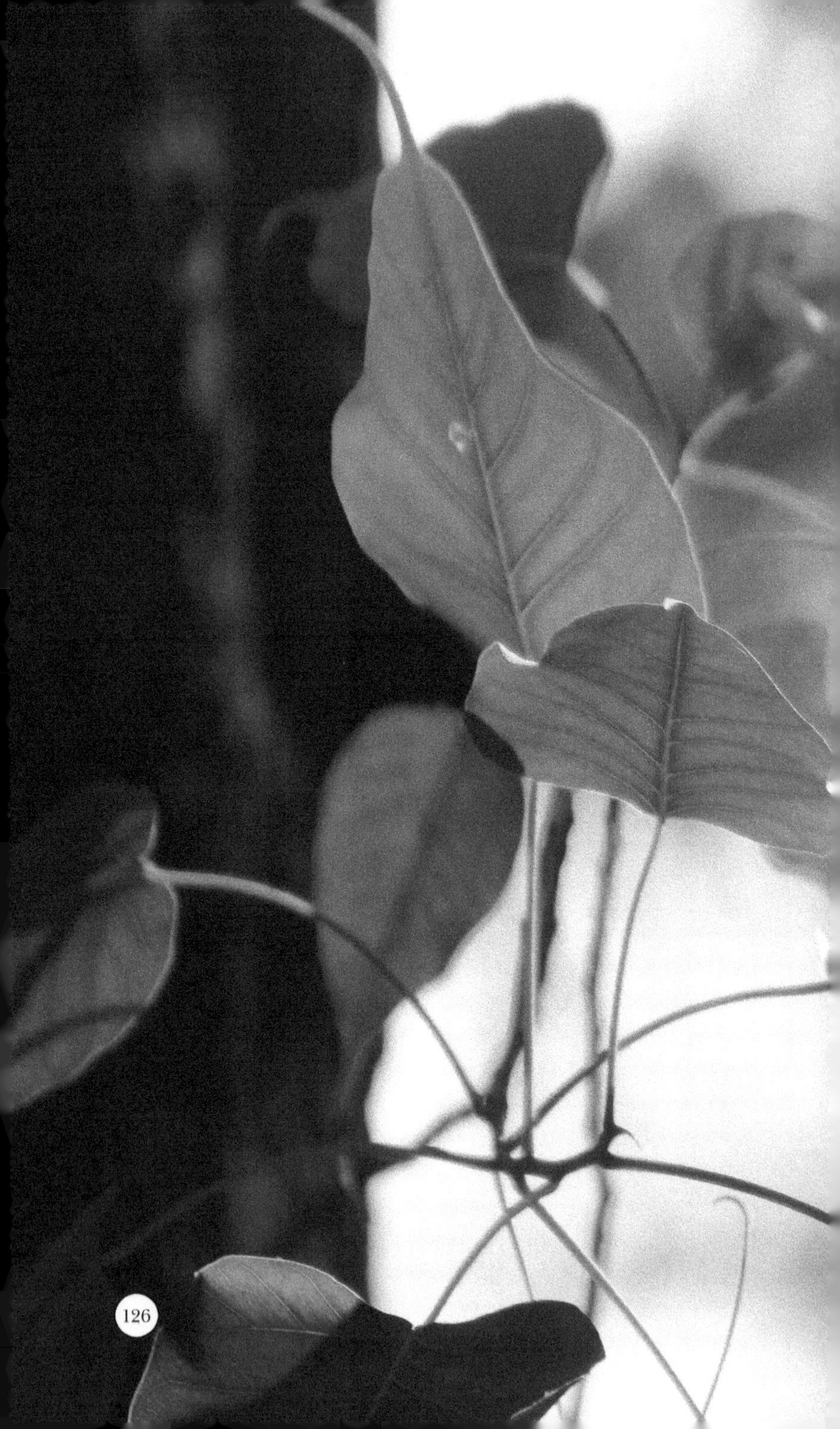

Seek not... that which comes with a craving to stay.

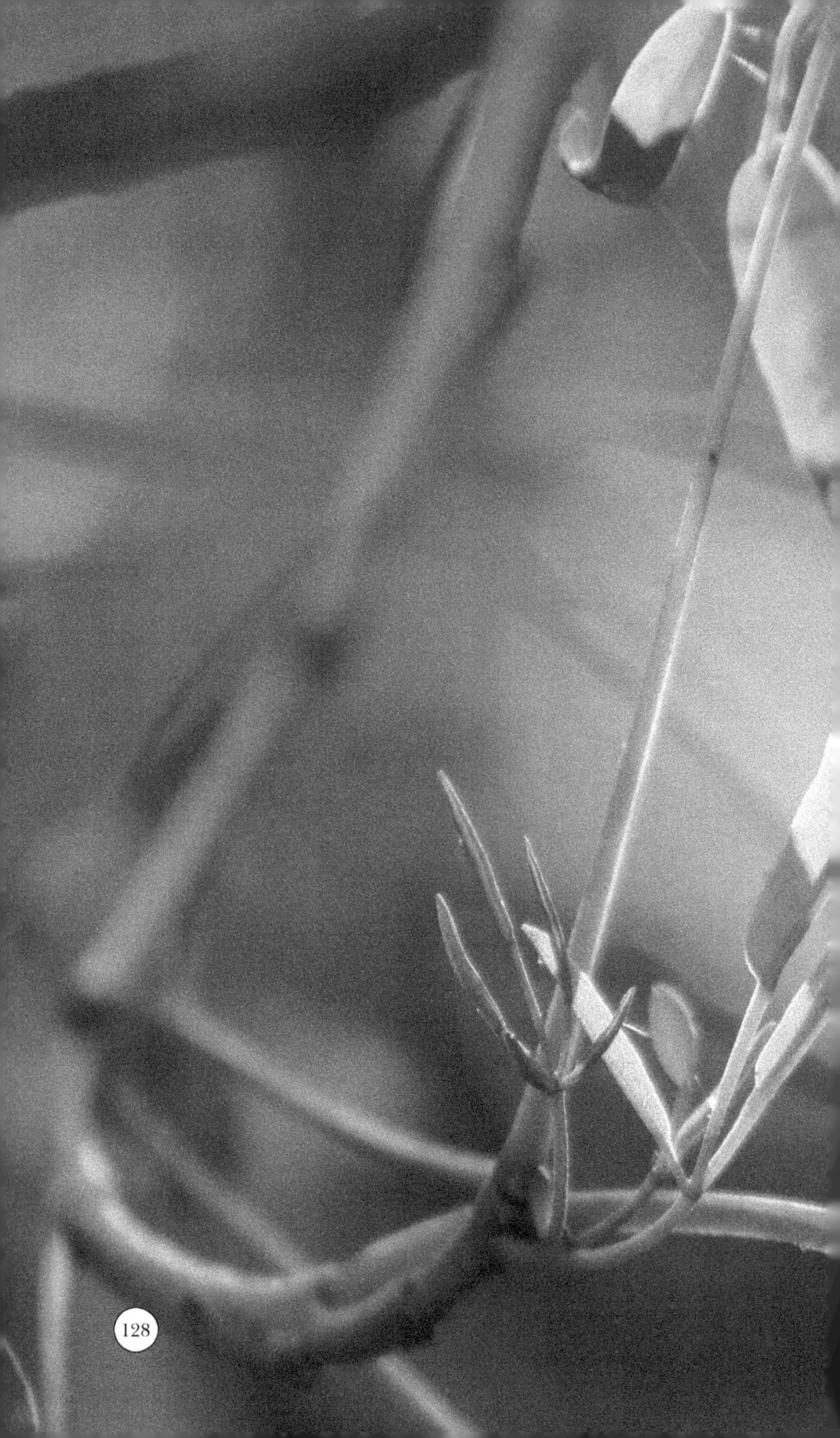

**Thus far... this wide...
is needed to truly
conquer the hearts.**

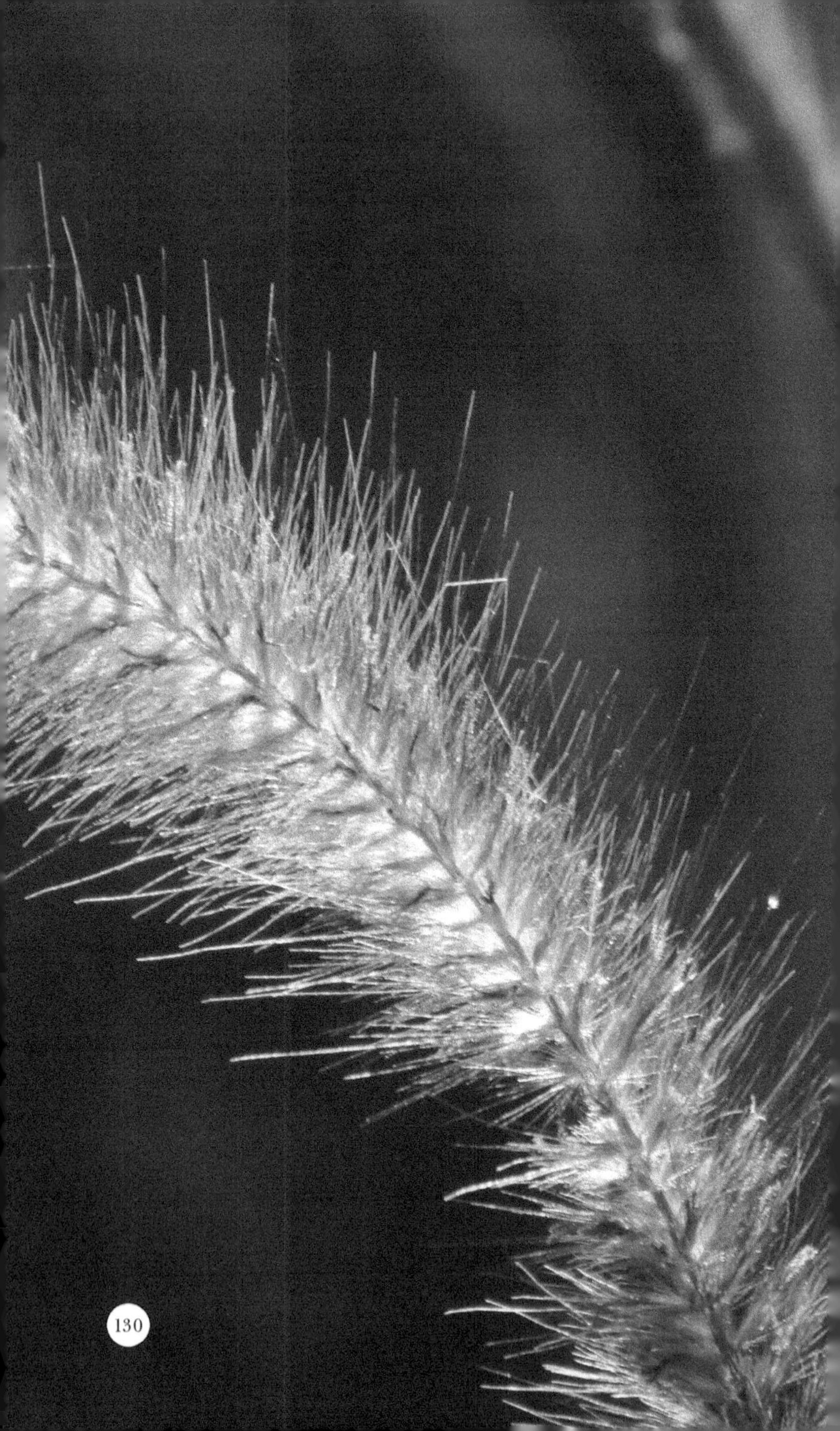

You might stagger into a path... that might illuminate your journey.

Can you look at a flower... and not partake in the wisdom it has to offer.

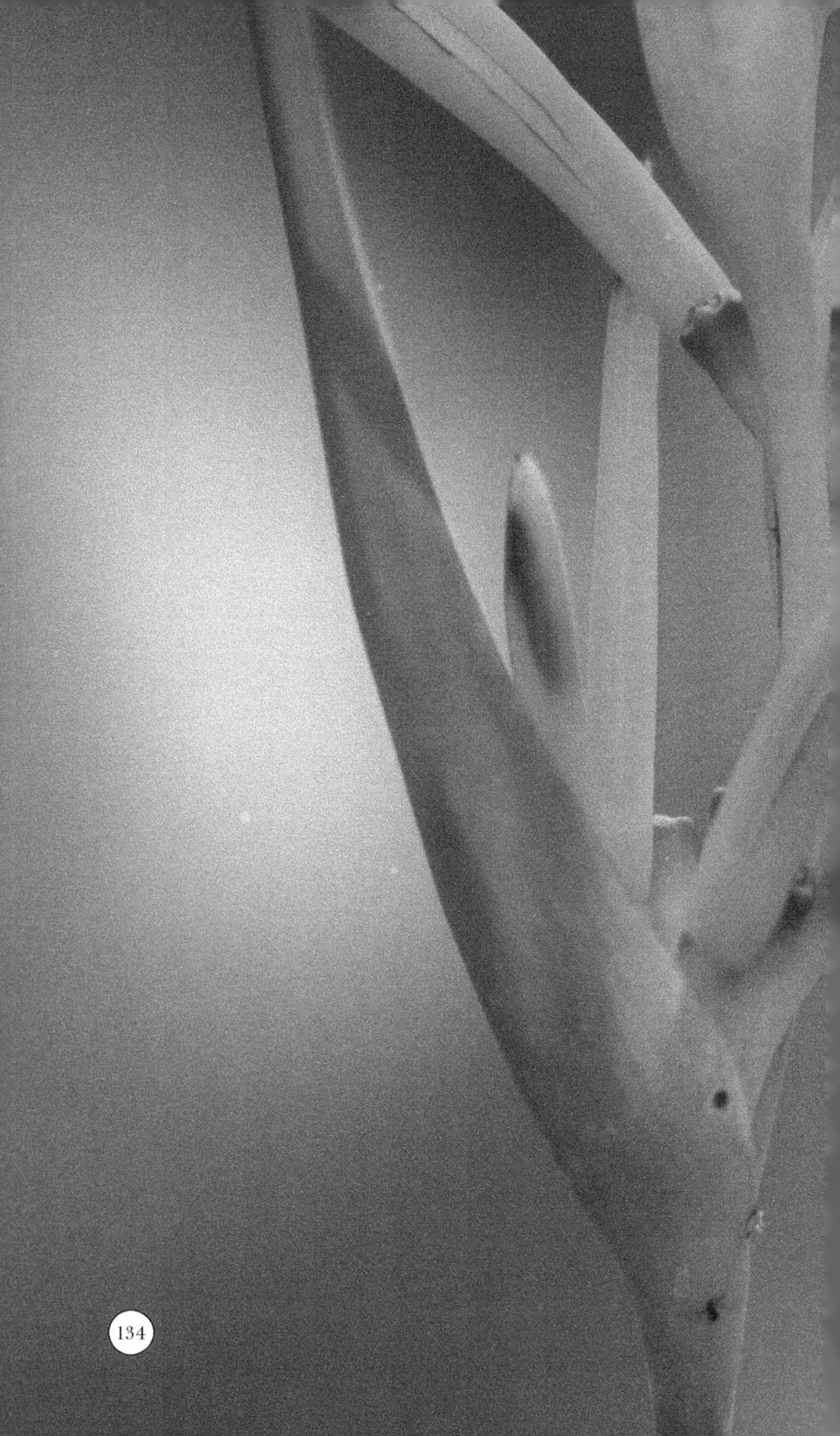

There is no greater strength... than the one that comes with your embracing service.

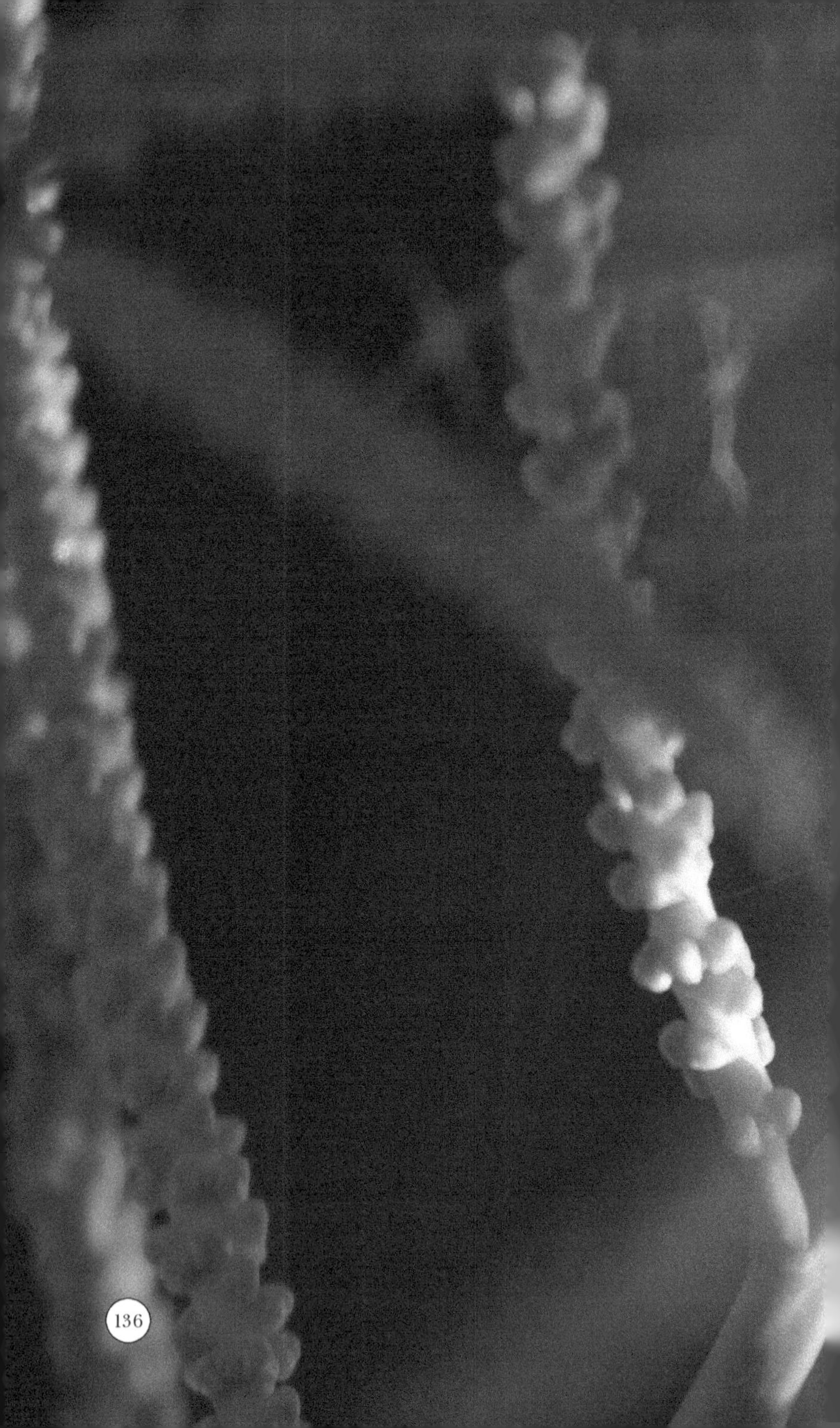

You can choose to be the one... who can share the brightness you see.

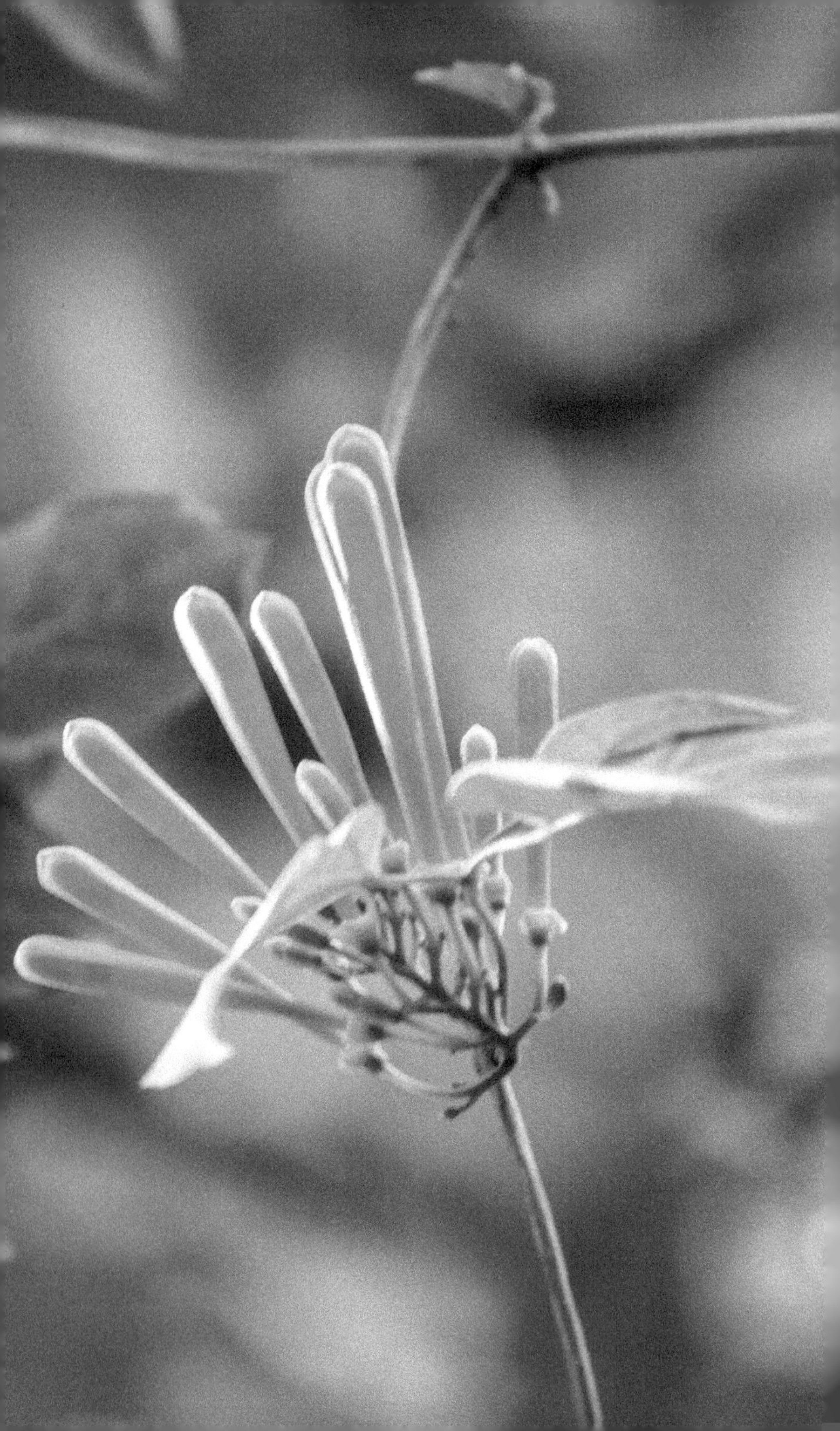

9 798889 724507 9